Photoshop 3.0: Knock Their Socks Off!

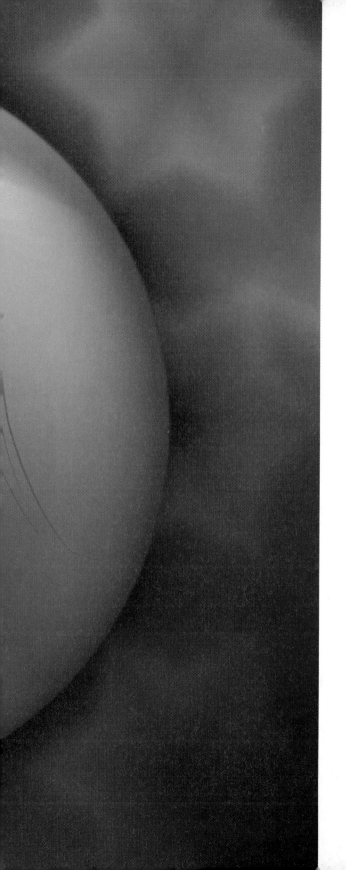

Photoshop 3.0: Knock Their Socks Off!

Peter Fink
with Foreword by Kai Krause

Ziff-Davis Press
Emeryville, California

Development Editors	Dan Brodnitz and Valerie Haynes Perry
Copy Editor	Kelly Green
Technical Reviewer	Dan Brodnitz
Project Coordinator	Cort Day
Proofreader	Carol Burbo
Cover Illustration	Regan Honda
Cover Design	Regan Honda
Series Design	Laura Lamar/MAX, San Francisco
Word Processing	Howard Blechman
Page Layout Artist	Bruce Lundquist
PrePress Color Correction	Joe Schneider
Indexer	Anne Leach

Ziff-Davis Press books are produced on a Macintosh computer system with the following applications: FrameMaker®, Microsoft® Word, QuarkXPress®, Adobe Illustrator®, Adobe Photoshop®, Adobe Streamline™, MacLink®*Plus*, Aldus® FreeHand™, Collage Plus™.

If you have comments or questions or would like to receive a free catalog, call or write:
Ziff-Davis Press
5903 Christie Avenue
Emeryville, CA 94608
1-800-688-0448

ISBN 1-56276-273-7

Manufactured in the United States of America
✪ This book is printed on paper that contains 50% total recycled fiber of which 20% is de-inked postconsumer fiber.
10 9 8 7 6 5 4 3 2

**This book is dedicated to
Pat Quinn, Nancy Selden,
and Sonja Siegel.
Thank you all for your
special contributions.**

TABLE OF CONTENTS

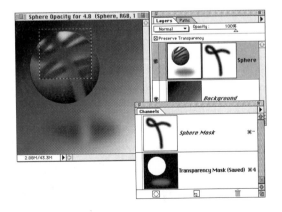

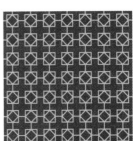

FOREWORD

Photoshop is one of those things, like Lego blocks, where you can put together components in so many ways that it's just not exhaustible. The fact that the combinatorics of all the tools in this Swiss Army Knife of software are so broad can be seen in the number of books that have appeared on the topic. I for one welcome this addition to the library with open arms. Not in the sense that they would replace one another, but there simply are so many angles from which to examine the topics. It's sheer endless!

Peter Fink has earned his rank amongst the Photoshoppers out there "the hard way." Many of you might have met him as he toured the country, giving seminars. This is what really endears me to Peter's work: It has an air of real grassroots problem-solving about it. Undoubtedly he has come across these issues and their solutions and seen actual humans struggle with the major brick walls as well as the smallish pebbles in the road.

This is a collection of tips, a mixture of The Big Idea and many more of The Neat Little Tricks. It's not a traditional "book on a software program," and it's not a rehash of the manual or an index of featuritis. Peter has made it topic-driven, facing the challenges with a focus and then providing answers with a variety of tools and methods.

It is the Methodology that shows Peter Fink's experience: a good use of color images to illustrate step by steps, some background without becoming too basic, some hidden tips without becoming elitist or esoteric. It's a fine balance to keep...

Many times a book can reflect the particular style and approach taken by the author, and that too can be a boon to finding nuggets. Peter is less projecting his own particular Finkesqueness (I gotta use these things), but rather paves a very wide path for users of all kinds.

I think there would be very few of the wide bell curve of users that would not readily find ideas and techniques scattered throughout this book. And that really has to be the final quantifier, if not qualifier: The price of admission here should be paid back even with just ONE idea that saves time or makes a client happy or solves a tricky problem...

To be sure, this is not light reading; it's not a novella. This is hands-on, read-and-play kind of material. You should expect to have your computer on most of the time, trying the techniques as you go. Hey, there'll be a pop quiz...be ready.

There is no shortcut to knowledge, of course. To truly internalize these precious recipes, it's not enough to display this book on your shelf; you will need the one road that gets you there, Experience. But it need not be learning by rote horror, dry and pragmatic. As you will find in these pages, here you have an area of knowledge where the path of getting there may be as much fun as having arrived...

I remember fondly finding all those tasty morsels of new combinations and wild effects, as well as the mundane "3 steps to a clean mask" utilities. At the time, three years ago, there was only one book available and much of the knowledge was yet to be revealed. It is gratifying to me to see some of it reaching ever-wider audiences and for authors like Peter to expand the envelope yet again. It was always my belief that with all the tools out there we simply have not seen more than an absolutely tiny fraction of the possible images lurking in our machines. Often what you see described in this book was simply not doable without either being a very dedicated specialist in some field or a very patient artist doing it in an analog fashion. No one, probably not even Peter himself, would have believed the contents of a book like this a decade ago.

With that thought in mind, these being the golden days, the new Renaissance, I hope you will enjoy this work and apply its contents in good spirits. You might be the next PhotoChopin!

Santa Barbara, Winter 1994, with warmest regards
Kai

ACKNOWLEDGMENTS

I admire authors who can draw a cast of dozens into a book project. This book proceeded with a cast of a handful of experts and participating companies.

Adobe Systems Incorporated provided invaluable assistance starting back in 1991. Thanks to John Kunze, Steve Guttman, and Russell Brown for their support and inside looks while I was an Adobe consultant, during the time this book began to germinate. Thanks also to Rita Amladi and Matt Brown for their help during the writing of the book, and thanks to Photoshop programmers Tom Knoll and Mark Hamburg, who offered technical comments that helped clear up critical questions.

Kai Krause kept the ball rolling, posting free technical tips about how to use Photoshop channel calculations on America Online starting in 1992. Kai's comments and support further illuminated this subject matter during my first Photoshop seminar series in 1993 and during the writing of this book. Kai's vision brings inspiration to us all, even when have no idea what he is saying (we figure it out later, though, you bet!).

Several people at Ziff-Davis Press played critical roles. Cindy Hudson had the faith to sign this book, and Eric Stone guided the project and expertly rode herd on its author. Valerie Haynes Perry delivered the book's consistent voice (as only an expert editor can) and toned down my rhetorical excesses. Thanks also to Dan Brodnitz for his editorial expertise and his capable handling of the critical Photoshop technical review. Cort Day, Charles Cowens, and the very capable design group produced the actual pages. Others who contributed without my knowledge of your names, thank you! It takes a lot of talented people to produce a good Photoshop book.

A group of select vendors generously provided material and deserve thanks. Adobe Systems Incorporated provided beta software and documentation for Photoshop 3.0, Andromeda Software Inc.,

HSC Software, and Xaos Tools provided third-party Photoshop filters. The photographic images in this book were graciously provided by PhotoDisc, and are Copyright 1994 by PhotoDisc, Inc., with the exception of the image of the girl with the painted face used in Chapters 6 and 7, which was photographed by Steve Kelly and appears on the Kodak Photo CD Sampler CD-ROM disc.

Finally, thanks to you, the reader, for buying this book, which I hope serves you well. Your support will make more books like this possible.

INTRODUCTION

This is a book for people who create commercial images for a living—a different kind of Photoshop book.

If you want a substitute for the manual, or a book to help you start to learn Photoshop, this isn't it. If you need a reference book that tells you about every menu choice, filter, button and knob, this isn't it either. If you're looking for a book to help you create surrealistic art, this might be it—but you won't find that sort of art here.

Ah, but if you're a working commercial artist who needs to sharpen your existing Photoshop skills, welcome! You'll find plenty you can use, because this is a book written with your needs in mind. It digs deeper into the topics you need (how to make a great-looking bevel edge or control the look of a metal surface), and omits the topics you probably don't need (how to make a green-dripping-lava moonscape).

This book assumes you're a pro, and that you've done your home-work. You've completed the standard Photoshop Tutorial, you're familiar with the manual, and you've worked for a while with the program. Now you need a deeper viewpoint, plus better techniques to use in your day-to-day work. They're here.

In addition to the techniques, we've provided explanations for areas of the program that often prove confusing. In combination with the explanations offered in your Photoshop manual, this infor-mation should help you work more efficiently.

It is said that art is long and time is fleeting. This has become even more true since the introduction of computers. I hope that with the help of this book, you'll be able to get home in time for dinner.

P A R T

Filling in the Gaps

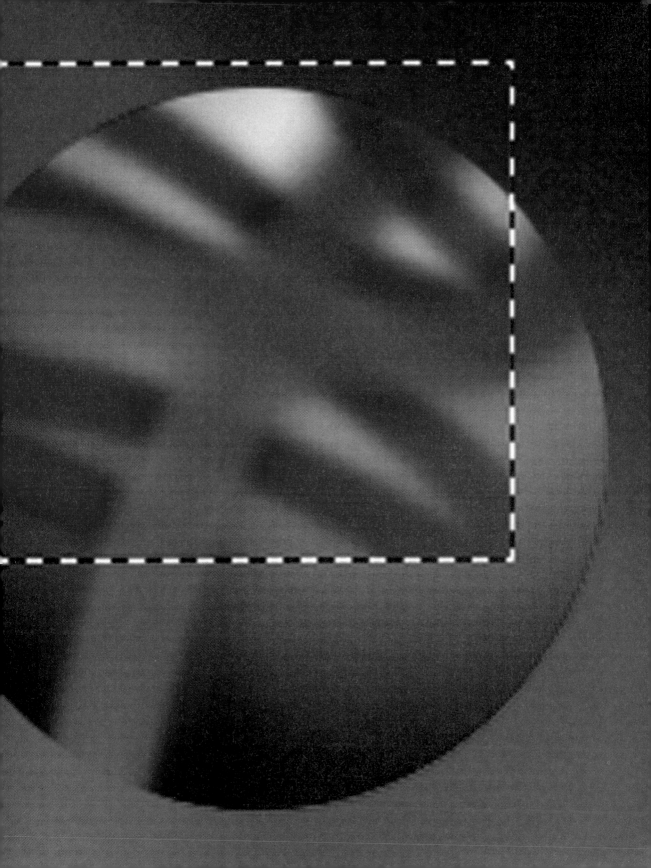

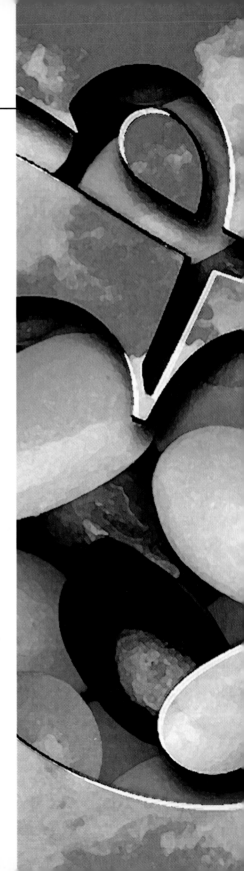

CHAPTER

A Photoshop Imaging Model

eneath its artistic exterior, the Adobe Photoshop program inhabits a complex mathematical universe. Fortunately for most of us, we don't work directly with the math—we relate to the program visually. This occasionally leads us into puzzling situations.

The first chapter of this book strives to clear up some of this puzzlement with a simplified Photoshop imaging model that describes how Photoshop works. In the interest of clarity, it cuts some mathematical corners. If your grasp of imaging technology is sound enough that you notice where the corners are cut, congratulations! You're ahead of the pack, and you probably know more than is needed to use Photoshop well.

Even if you're a fairly advanced user of Photoshop, however, you might never have taken time to consider how Photoshop constructs an image. A firm sense of how images are constructed will always help you work better in Photoshop. For this reason, the model established in this chapter applies to the techniques that are covered throughout this book.

The imaging model consists of the following elements:

- Pixels

- Bitmaps

- Dithers or halftones

- Masks

- Grayscale

- Color images

- Calculations

- Layers

Pixel Graphics versus Vector Graphics

Today's computers work with two broad varieties of images: pixel (picture element) graphics and vector graphics. Pixel images are ideal for reproducing photographs and other images that contain large amounts of unstructured detail. Photoshop is a pixel-graphics program that can also use some very handy PostScript language features (Figure 1.1).

Figure 1.1
A simple vector graphic (left) is based on a compact computer description of straight lines and curves. A pixel image (right) is less compact but better suited to the reproduction of random photolike detail. Photoshop produces pixel images.

Common PostScript illustration programs like Adobe Illustrator, Aldus Freehand, and CorelDRAW! are examples of vector-graphics programs. Vector graphics are mathematical descriptions of shapes that can be built from straight lines and curves. Computer illustration programs create such graphics, which are also used for the letterforms in modern computer fonts. Vector graphics are compact and highly portable, and they can be greatly enlarged or reduced at will with no visible ill effects. These graphics are written in special computer languages (if you work in commercial graphics and print, PostScript is very probably the language your computer uses), and must be translated into human-visible form by specialized computers called interpreters.

In contrast, pixel graphics require less translation, but their files can be very large.

Bitmaps and Pixel Grids

The simplest type of computer image is the black-and-white bitmap. It shares many characteristics with every Photoshop image. The bitmap also shares characteristics with the simplest mosaics, which trick the eye into seeing an image instead of a collection of small tiles (Figure 1.2). Early computer imaging researchers relied on the fundamentals of simple mosaics:

- The image is built from picture elements, or pixels, arrayed on a regular grid.

Figure 1.2
A mosaic (left) and a computer bitmap (right) are both built of picture elements arrayed on a regular grid.

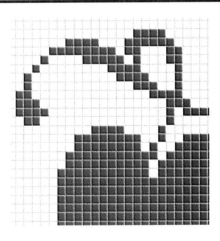

- The greater the number of pixels and the smaller they are, the more detail is evident in the picture.

- Once the eye no longer sees the individual picture elements, it sees only the image they create.

Tapestries, pointillistic artwork, the big image displays in Times Square and ballparks, and commercial printers' halftone screens (to name just a few) also rely on the same visual principle: Once the picture elements become small enough, the eye sees just the image.

The Characteristics of Pixels

The smaller the pixels that make up an image, the greater the detail these pixels can resolve, and the greater the detail, the higher the image's *resolution* (Figure 1.3). Photoshop defines this resolution in terms of pixels per centimeter or pixels per inch. For example, a moderately high-resolution Photoshop image might contain 300 pixels per inch (300 ppi). Due to the tyranny of simple arithmetic, as pixel size decreases it takes a lot more pixels to make up an image of a given size. This is why Photoshop high-resolution images have large computer file sizes.

Pixel-graphics programs impose stricter constraints on the positioning and brightness of their picture elements than do mosaics, tapestries, and the like. The most fundamental of these constraints are the following:

- Pixels are arrayed on a rigid grid, as if they were occupying squares on graph paper.

- In bitmaps, these pixels are binary, which means they are either on or off.

- Binary pixels can only represent two levels of gray: black or white.

Figure 1.4 illustrates a bitmap's pixel grid.

Figure 1.3

As pixels become smaller, image resolution and the ability to show detail increase. With its fixed tiles, a mosaic (left) has a fixed resolution. Computer bitmaps can have a variety of resolutions (center and right).

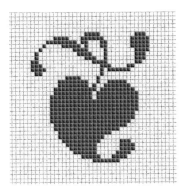  

Figure 1.4

A bitmap's pixel grid is rarely shown, but it is always in effect. In Photoshop you can read each pixel's address on the grid by its x and y positions.

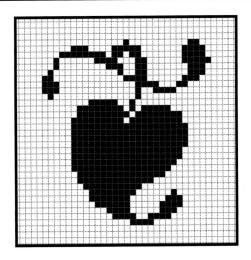

The grid arrangement allows each pixel to have its own *address,* expressed as x and y graph coordinates. Pixel addresses let the computer locate individual pixels so it can compare images pixel-by-pixel and superimpose multiple images precisely. As we will see, such operations make it possible for Photoshop to create full-color images.

In a Dither

People quickly tire of looking at just black and white. At the very least they want a few shades of gray in a photographic image. In a bitmap image it's possible to arrange the black or white pixels in such a way that the eye perceives shades of gray. This is called dithering (Figure 1.5). Dithering sacrifices detail in exchange for these artificial grays, but in a simple grid-based bitmap image there's no other way to give the perception of tones between black and white.

Figure 1.5
By grouping pixels in a dither, a bitmap gives the impression of grays in exchange for detail. Many different kinds of dithers are used in computer graphics.

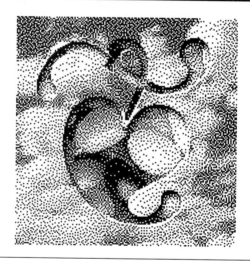

Frisket Masks

When you mask something, you protect it. A *frisket* is a mask of thin paper that can be placed over an illustration to shield certain sections when using an airbrush. This book borrows the term frisket and calls the simplest Photoshop masks *frisket masks*. You can use a frisket mask to define some regions as completely masked and others as unprotected. This approach allows you to limit an edit to a desired region. Figure 1.6 illustrates how an outline mask can be used to edit a bitmap image.

Figure 1.6
A mask allows you to limit an edit to a specified region. When loaded as the selection into the bitmap image at left and filled with black, the outline mask at the center produces the edited bitmap image at right.

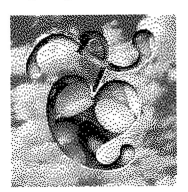  

By default, a Photoshop mask is light in areas you intend to edit, and dark in areas you wish to protect. You can reverse this convention if you like, making the mask light in the protected areas. Examples and explanations in this book assume the default mask settings.

Grayscale

Bitmaps reigned on Macintosh computers for a few early years in the MacPaint program, but Apple eventually moved on to better things. Building on the foundation of bitmaps, computer technology took the next logical step to grayscale images, where pixels have intermediate levels of brightness. This allows pixels to reproduce graytones directly, reducing or eliminating the need for on-screen dithering.

Bytes and Shades of Gray

The first grayscale systems allowed only a few intermediate levels of gray between black and white. Within a year or two this increased to the PostScript maximum of 256 gray levels. This maximum makes possible continuous tone (or *contone*) reproduction, which creates a visually smooth tone from black all the way to white (Figure 1.7).

Figure 1.7
Grayscale images can have different numbers of gray levels. The severely posterized image at the left has just four levels of gray—black, white, and two intermediate levels. The image at the right has 256 levels of gray, more than enough to give the impression of continuous tone.

Since computers are binary beasts, the number of gray shades (including black and white) has always been tied to powers of two; 256 is two raised to the eighth power. Thus it takes 8 binary bits to store a pixel's brightness level (the 8-bit *byte* is standard in much of computing). This is why Photoshop's grayscale images are often called eight-bit grayscale images. Eight-bit grayscale is about as complex as things get for Photoshop at its most basic pixel level. This is because Photoshop color images are coordinated groups of 8-bit grayscale images.

Halftones

Laser printers and imagesetters are also binary beasts. For example, the toner most printers use is black, not gray. To print out images, all the laser printer can do is apply this toner in some places and not apply it in others. Still, there has to be some way to get all those nice intermediate levels of gray onto the printed page. This is where halftones come in.

Halftoning is a dithering mechanism that uses solid halftone dots to simulate tonal values between solid and clear. Halftone dots aren't really pixels; they are *made up* of pixels. As a result, they vary in size and shape and, at high resolutions, can simulate subtle and convincing tonal gradations. If your printer or press uses color inks, halftoning will yield a variety of colors. If your printer or press uses black inks, halftoning will generate convincing grays.

Although it's possible to specify halftones in Photoshop, your output service bureau usually handles this task. Your halftoning plans will influence your choice of resolution. Like the dithering used for bitmaps, halftoning sacrifices some detail in exchange for tone. Standard halftone systems generally yield the best results when you use an image resolution that's 1.5 to 2 times the lines-per-inch ruling of your halftone screen.

The new stochastic screening systems sacrifice less detail in their dithering and therefore require less resolution to get a similar result.

The technology of halftoning is maddeningly complex, but in practice, you rarely need to worry about it. Halftoning tends to take care of itself nicely without your direct intervention once you've made it clear which type of halftoning you want.

Contone Masks

A mask can contain intermediate levels of brightness between black and white. Since in Photoshop the light areas of a mask permit change, where a mask contains intermediate levels of brightness it allows intermediate degrees of change (Figure 1.8). A grayscale mask can be a continuous-tone image, a frisket mask with no intermediate gray levels, or anything in between. Photoshop allows you to store grayscale masks in *alpha channels,* which in effect are auxiliary grayscale images of the same dimensions (width and height in pixels) as the main image. Most of the techniques described in this book rely on such masks and alpha channels in one way or another.

Figure 1.8
A Photoshop mask can contain up to 256 levels of gray, making continuous-tone (contone) masks possible. When loaded as the selection into the grayscale image at left and then filled with black, the contone mask at center produces the edited grayscale image at right.

Masks, Channels, and Selections

Due to ambiguous terminology and frequent substitution of one term for another in casual conversation and writing, there's plenty of confusion among Photoshop users about masks, channels, and selections. Simply put, you store a mask in a channel. To use this mask you load it, at which point it becomes the current selection, which you then edit. However, due to Photoshop's flexibility, many possible variations on this theme still exist. Chapter 2 discusses this topic in detail.

Color Images, Calculations, and Layers

After grayscale images, color was the next logical step in computer image technology. Color represents a technical leap for computer hardware, but from the standpoint of programs like Photoshop it boils down to coordinating three or four grayscale images.

Color Images

A Photoshop color image consists of three or four "color" channels in addition to the alpha channels used for storing masks (Figure 1.9). Each color channel is really a grayscale image whose brightness levels equal various color quantities in Photoshop's various color modes. In the case of an RGB image, for example, each channel's brightness level directly converts to the level of one of the image's color components (red, green, or blue). If you examine the individual color channels, you'll find that they contain brightness levels that match the color levels of the color pixels (Figure 1.10).

Figure 1.9
Photoshop's Channels palette shows you both color channels and alpha channels. In this CMYK image, channels 1 through 4 are the color channels, each of which is a grayscale image. Although it appears in the palette for convenience, channel 0 isn't a true channel—it's a composite view of the color channels.

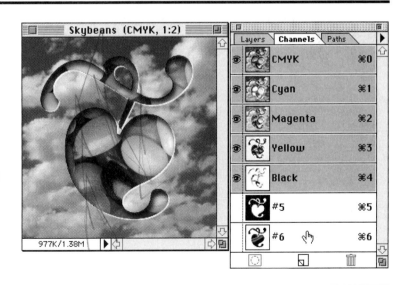

Figure 1.10
In an RGB image, channel brightness levels convert directly to color component levels for red, green, and blue. Here the Eyedropper is sampling the pixel near the arrow's tip. The Info palette is displaying the pixel's levels and its x and y coordinates on the pixel address grid.

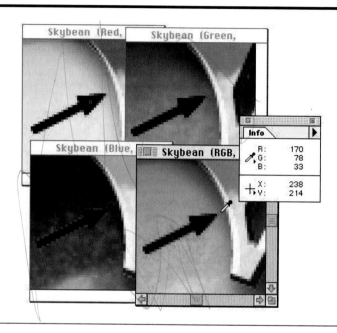

Photoshop displays color on your screen for your convenience only. You only see the color in your image when the color components are combined in some way: by Photoshop on your display screen, by a color printer, or on a color proof or press sheet, for example. In reality there is no color within an image file, just a collection of grayscale "color" channels. When you call for a change in color, Photoshop modifies the brightness values in the color channels, then uses the modified values to adjust the displayed color.

Calculations

Since each pixel in each channel has a brightness level, and since each pixel has an address, the computer can easily perform arithmetic with the brightness levels in any channel of an image. To illustrate this point, in a Photoshop RGB image you can select the pixel at address x = 10, y = 12, have Photoshop add the brightness values of the red channel and an alpha channel at that address, and put the resulting sum into the same address in any channel—even a brand new one. This may sound like stodgy Mrs. McGillicuddy's dreaded eighth-grade algebra class, but when you start doing Photoshop calculations with millions of pixels the visual results can be stunning. For example, multiplying two grayscale channels together is like placing transparencies of the two channels on a light table and viewing them in register (Figure 1.11). Automated process-camera work! Who would have known?

Figure 1.11
One of the most useful channel calculations for mask construction is the multiply command. When multiplied together, the two channels (left and center) look like two transparencies viewed in register on a light table. The result (right) can be saved in any channel, including a new one.

Layers

Keeping track of millions of pixels occupies a great deal of computer memory and processing power. Until recently this limited small computers to working with a single layer of pixels. In Photoshop, once an edit was made, the pixels were changed, and that was that. Unless you chose to immediately undo an edit, the only way to retrieve an earlier version of the image was to open an earlier file or revert, discarding all edits made since the last save.

As fast PowerPC and Pentium computers have come on the market, it has become feasible to expand Photoshop's features once again. The dominant new feature of Photoshop 3.0 is Layers: multiple co-ordinated color images. Each layer acts something like a clear sheet of acetate with a portion of your image on it—but you can vary the opacity of the layer and even assign it a grayscale transparency mask (Figure 1.12).

Figure 1.12
Layers allows you to experiment freely. Each layer can be super-imposed on the image with any desired opacity using the program's several painting modes. Here a new chrome shape and drop shadow are added as separate layers. The original image remains unchanged as the background.

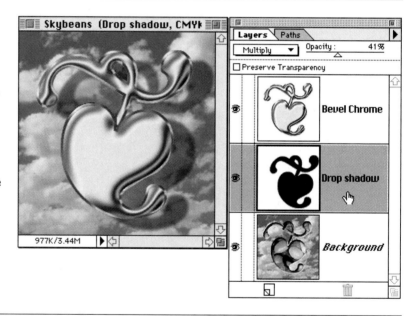

Layers allows much more flexibility and experimentation than was possible with earlier versions of Photoshop, without causing huge changes in the imaging model. Layers also uses more memory and requires more processing power than did earlier versions of Photoshop, but this is nothing new in computer graphics, which renders hardware obsolete at the rate of about one generation of computer technology per year.

Summary

The imaging model presented in this chapter is an attempt to synthesize the perspectives of graphics professionals regarding the nuts and bolts of the overall process. In the interest of providing a clear sense of what's under the hood, I've provided a paradigm that serves this purpose. While no two graphic artists would arrive at the exact same scheme, perhaps we can all agree on the basics.

CHAPTER

2

Masks, Selections, and Alpha Channels

Traditional Masks

Photoshop Selections, Masks, and Alpha Channels

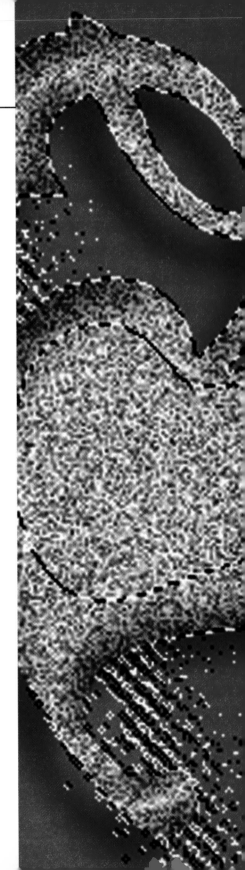

Most of the effects in this book require masks. Adobe Photoshop is a powerful masking program, and Photoshop 3.0's new Layers function increases this power significantly. However, because Layers also reduces the need for certain types of masks, you might hear (and be inclined to believe) that masks aren't really needed anymore. Resist this inclination and instead realize that using masks with Layers will expand your opportunities to experiment and produce pleasing results. Chapter 4 discusses the Layers function in depth.

Before you can fully appreciate Photoshop's masking tools, you need to know something about masks in general. This chapter offers a brief overview of some traditional types of masks. It then offers a structured way to think about Photoshop masks, selections, and alpha channels. This approach will help you create, use, modify, and store masks, which you can then use to control the edits you make to images.

Traditional Masks

A mask protects part of an image. The degree of protection can be complete or partial. In traditional graphic-arts settings, artists, prepress specialists, and photographers have used masks in different forms for many years. This section provides an overview of the two major categories of masks: those that define outlines and those that contain tone.

Category One: Masks that Define Outlines

The first category of traditional mask includes stencils, frisket masks, and lithographic films. As you will see, it's helpful to use the name *frisket mask* as a general term that describes the Photoshop equivalent of these traditional tools. These masks are made up of open regions and protected regions. Both regions have well-defined outlines with hard edges. When the image is changed by the application of paint or by photographic exposure, the clear regions are altered while the protected regions remain unchanged.

Stencils

The most basic mask is a *stencil* (Figure 2.1). In the open areas of a stencil you can apply paint; in the other areas, the stencil totally protects the underlying image. Most people consider a stencil a fairly crude heavy-duty mask designed for repeated use in standard circumstances, often to paint simple words or symbols.

Figure 2.1
A stencil (left) is a very basic form of mask, which is often used for relatively crude marking tasks (right).

Frisket Masks

Carrying the stencil principle to finer work, a frisket mask is made of thinner material that allows finer detail in the outline. An example is the frisket mask material used by airbrush artists when they need a well-defined edge. The artist places an adhesive-backed sheet of frisket material directly on the image surface, carefully cuts away the desired outline with a knife, and then uses the airbrush to apply paint to the exposed area (Figure 2.2).

Figure 2.2
A frisket mask protects areas of artwork during airbrushing (left). When the frisket is removed, the outline emerges (right).

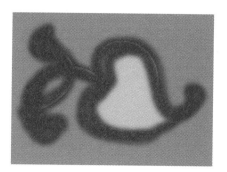 

Lithographic Films

The photographic, or *lithographic*, film used for prepress production is designed to deliver the highest possible contrast. It registers only clear and black. All outlines have hard edges, and all tones between black and white are represented by solid halftone dots.

In the preparation of traditional mechanicals, production artists can use rubylith or amberlith material to create masks. This material consists of an acetate support sheet coated with a thin layer of red or orange material, which appears opaque to lithographic film. With a knife the artist scores the desired outline into the surface material and peels it away, producing a mask that's ready for the process camera (Figure 2.3).

In the process-camera and film-duplicating rooms of printing plants, detailed lithographic masks are made in the course of almost every printing job. They're not called masks, they're called films for making printing plates—but the principles are the same.

Figure 2.3
On a traditional mechanical (left), red or amber lithographic masking material indicates areas to be made solid on final film for platemaking (right).

Knock type out of amberlith

Category Two: Masks that Contain Tone

The second category of traditional masks contains intermediate tones, or shades of gray, made possible by using normal-contrast photographic film. These masks, also called contone masks, include photographic special-effects masks and photographic tone and detail masks.

Photographic Special-Effects Masks

Shoot an out-of-focus copy of a hard-edged lithographic mask on normal-contrast photographic film, and you'll get a mask with a feathered edge. With a combination of lithographic film, regular film, various sandwiching tricks, and exposure and focus adjustments, it is possible to create numerous photographic special-effects masks (Figure 2.4).

Many of the finished image examples in this book could have been produced by photographic methods—given enough time and resources. In many cases, the images would have required many hours of special-effects photography and budgets of hundreds or thousands of dollars.

Figure 2.4
Using various tricks of the trade, a special-effects photographer can combine a defocused negative (left) with positive line art (center) to give a special-effects mask (right), in this case an outglow mask.

Photoshop allows you to apply proven photographic mask techniques in electronic form. Part 2 of this book illustrates several of the most popular effects.

Photographic Tone and Detail Masks

Photographers and prepress specialists have used photographic masks for decades to adjust the color, tone, and detail of images. These types of masks have often been named according to their function: color-separation masks, bump masks, highlight masks, shadow masks, and so on. These are often modified versions of the very images they are used to change (Figure 2.5).

The possible uses of masks with photographs are endless and include some of the most technically sophisticated photographic effects. By skillfully adjusting the tonal content of the mask, it is possible to accomplish changes that might not have seemed possible on first examination. When they are well used, tone and detail masks leave no evidence; those who view the final product notice only the image itself.

Figure 2.5
In the photo at the left the sky is rather flat. Using a pin-register system and a composite mask (center) the photographer can double-expose just the clouds during photographic printing to get the image at right.

Due to the level of knowledge and the amount of time required to prepare color, tone, and detail masks, they are most commonly used in special circumstances and advanced cases. Photoshop's quick and predictable control simplifies the process and makes experimentation easier and more affordable. This book uses the Photoshop equivalents of these kinds of masks in Chapters 6 and 7.

Photoshop Selections, Masks, and Alpha Channels

The graphic arts industry consists of thousands of small independent firms that have their own ways of naming things, so mask terminology has never been entirely consistent. Not surprisingly, Photoshop masking terms can be confusing, which makes it more difficult than necessary to understand how the program works with masks. In Photoshop parlance a mask in active use is called a selection. The Photoshop term *mask* is reserved for an inactive selection stored in an alpha channel. This book doesn't strive to change the Adobe terminology, but for clarity we will coin a term or two as we go along.

Photoshop Frisket Masks

Among the key tools that this book will stress are Photoshop selections and the alpha channel masks that these selections can generate. There is no standard Adobe or graphic arts word that describes this kind of mask. Because these masks are similar in concept and operation to the masks that airbrush artists use, this book calls this type of Photoshop mask frisket masks.

Selections

You can use various tools and commands in Photoshop to select pixels of an image for editing. The moment you create a Photoshop selection you have a mask on your hands. The brightness values of this mask aren't immediately visible, but its composition is indicated (as well as possible) by the selection marquee (casually known as the marching ants).

Whenever you encounter the Photoshop term *selection*, think *currently active mask*. Adobe doesn't use this phrase, but as you'll see, it's a useful way to clarify the relationship between selections and masks (Figure 2.6). It will also help you to remember that selections and masks approach the same result from opposite perspectives. In any image, *selected* pixels are the pixels that are not masked and *masked* pixels are the pixels that are not selected.

A Way to Think of Selections

When you select a region, Photoshop uses a special area of memory to store the selection. For this discussion, we'll call this area the *selection buffer*. The selection buffer holds pixels whose brightness

Figure 2.6
The Leaf mask in Channel 5 has been loaded as the selection, becoming in effect the currently active mask. The selection marquee traces the outline of the selected area (the area not masked).

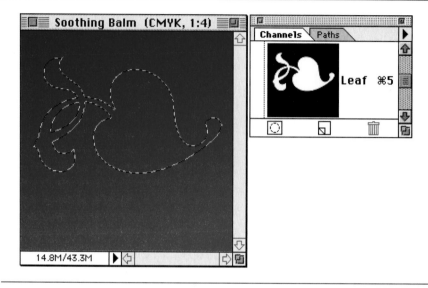

defines the size, shape, and scope of the selection itself. In effect, the selection buffer acts as a dedicated special-purpose channel: It holds a grayscale image of precisely the same pixel dimensions as the main image, and in indirect ways you can use it as you would use any other channel. (Channels are discussed later in this chapter.)

Think of the selection buffer as a mask through which all Photoshop edits must pass whenever a selection is active (Figure 2.7). In regions where the selection buffer contains pixels that are not white, the image is masked—the darker the pixels, the greater the masking. Strictly speaking, for any pixel in a Photoshop image, edits occur in proportion to the brightness of the corresponding pixel in the selection buffer (Figure 2.8). Adobe refers to regions that are shades of gray in the selection buffer as *partially selected*, the inverse of partially masked.

Figure 2.7
A selection occupies an area of memory this book calls the selection buffer. The buffer acts like a mask (center) through which all edits must pass before they can affect the image (right).

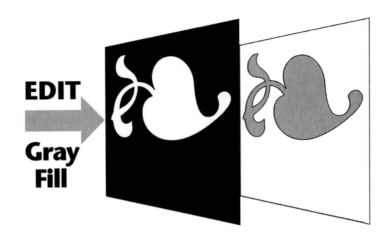

Figure 2.8
The brightness of pixels in the selection buffer determines the degree to which edits are performed on corresponding pixels in the main image.

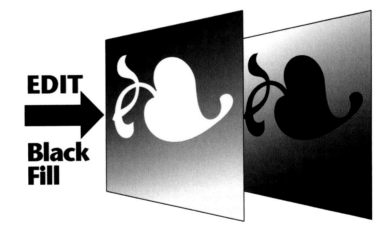

This selection-buffer model clarifies other important selection concepts:

■ When you apply the Load command, Photoshop transfers the contents of the specified alpha channel into the selection buffer (Figure 2.9). (This also holds true for the numerous other commands and key shortcuts you can use to load a selection.)

Figure 2.9
When you apply the Load command, Photoshop transfers the contents of the specified alpha channel into the selection buffer.

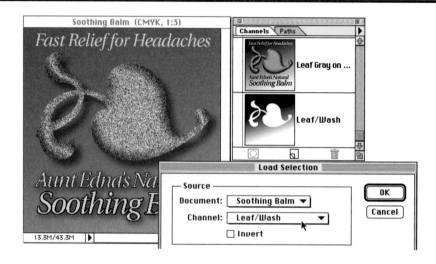

- In Quick Mask mode, Photoshop shows you the contents of the selection buffer overlaid on the image, and allows you to edit the selection buffer directly (Figure 2.10).

- The Inverse command inverts the contents of the selection buffer, just as the Invert command inverts the contents of a grayscale channel (Figure 2.11).

- When you perform a calculation (as we will see in Chapter 3) and specify that the result become a selection, Photoshop places the result of the calculation into the selection buffer instead of placing it in a channel.

- A floating selection becomes, in effect, a separate image that you can move and edit without affecting the underlying image. Edits still pass through the selection buffer as you work with the floating selection. These changes are not applied to the underlying image until you Defloat, or drop the floating selection.

Figure 2.10
In Quick Mask mode, Photoshop shows you the contents of the selection buffer overlaid on the image (top), and allows you to edit the selection buffer directly. When you return to Standard mode, the selection becomes active again (bottom).

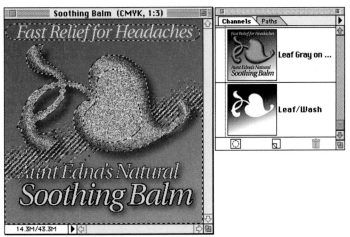

- With only the marching-ants marquee at its disposal, Photoshop has very limited means with which to indicate complex selections. The results can look misleading. The marching ants attempt to show the contents of the selection buffer by tracing the brightness level of 127 like an elevation contour map. Where the selection buffer contains gray information, the marquee is forced to

Figure 2.11
Applying the Inverse command to a selection (top) inverts the contents of the selection buffer. Here, the inverted selection buffer has been made visible via Quick Mask mode (bottom).

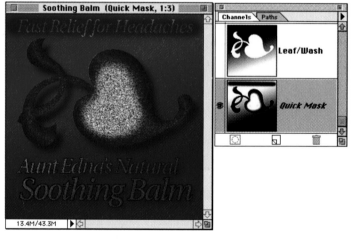

approximate. With practice and experimentation, you'll get used to reading these selections and editing accordingly (Figure 2.12). Note that when the Use Dot Gain for Grayscale checkbox in the Printing Inks dialog box is checked, a level different than 127 is traced. The level depends on the Dot Gain setting.

Figure 2.12
Here the image itself has been loaded into the selection buffer. Where the image is lighter, the marquee indicates a selection. Where the image is darker, no selection is visible. In fact, all pixels brighter than black will be affected by an edit of this selection.

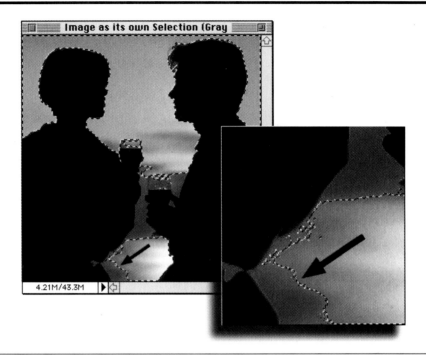

Selection Tools and Commands

There are many ways to create and modify selections in Adobe Photoshop. The Photoshop manual offers detailed descriptions of the tools, commands, and filters used for this purpose, which take three basic approaches (see Figure 2.13):

- The Marquee, Lasso, Pen, and Type tools let you create a frisket-style selection directly.

- When you use the Magic Wand tool and the Grow, Similar, Color Range and related commands and filters, Photoshop uses brightness information in one or more channels of the image to define a frisket-style selection.

- Using various anti-aliasing and feathering options, you can control the softness of the selection edges as the selections are made.

Figure 2.13a
Selection tools let you create an outline selection directly. You can, for example, convert a Pen-tool Path into a selection.

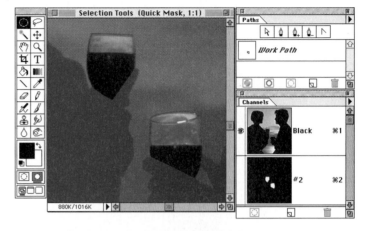

Figure 2.13b
Selection tools also let you create a selection based on brightness levels. One way is to apply the Magic Wand with anti-aliasing.

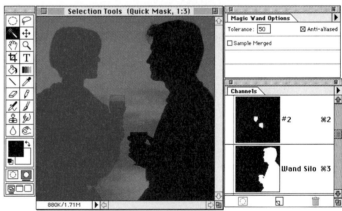

Figure 2.13c
Selection tools also let you control the softness of the outline edges. As with anti-aliasing, feathering can be applied as selections are made or after the fact. In this example, the Magic Wand selection has been feathered and saved in a new channel; then the selection has been edited further in Quick Mask mode.

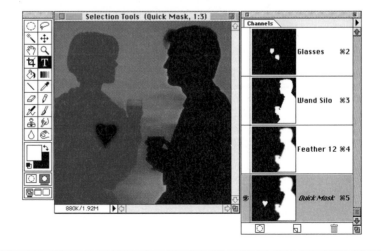

Adobe's Definition of a Photoshop Mask

In Adobe's Photoshop terminology, a mask is a selection that is saved in a channel. In other words, when you save a selection, Photoshop places the contents of the selection buffer in the channel you designate. When at some later time you load the channel that contains the selection (perhaps after making some modifications to the channel's grayscale image), Photoshop puts the channel's contents into the selection buffer.

In the preceding discussion we've seen that Photoshop masks and selections are close to being interchangeable; the only distinction is where the grayscale selection data resides and whether it currently affects edits. If the data resides in the selection buffer it is active and Adobe calls it a selection; if it resides in an alpha channel, it is stored and Adobe calls it a mask.

Photoshop Alpha Channels

In too many articles, discussions, and sometimes even books, the separate topics of masks, selections, and alpha channels get haphazardly lumped together as "channels," leading perfectly intelligent people to regard channels as deep and mysterious terrain. Actually, alpha channels are simply the Photoshop system for managing masks.

Given the preceding information on masks and selections, the otherwise intimidating subject of Photoshop channels boils down to a few simple points:

■ Photoshop allows up to 24 channels in an image file, including color channels. An alpha channel is any channel other than the color channels and the Channel Zero composite view.

■ The contents of any alpha channel can be loaded as the selection.

■ All alpha channels are created equal.

■ In addition to letting you load alpha channels as selections, Photoshop lets you view, edit, store, move, and apply calculations to them. Figures 2.14–2.18 illustrate this last point. Chapter 3 discusses channel calculations and filters that you will use often in building masks.

If you are unfamiliar with how to view channels overlaid on one another or how to edit one channel while viewing additional ones, this would be a good time to review the pertinent material in your Photoshop manual.

Figure 2.14
The Channels palette makes it easy to view all the channels in a document, with thumbnails of a size you choose. This is the color composite view, in which all four color channels of this CMYK image are chosen for editing.

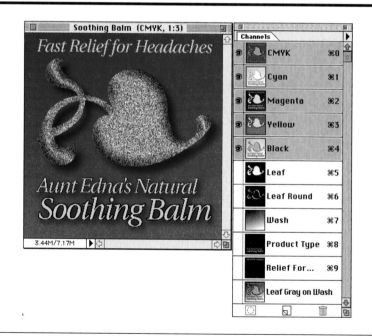

Figure 2.15
The Channels palette lets you view channels and make them active for editing.

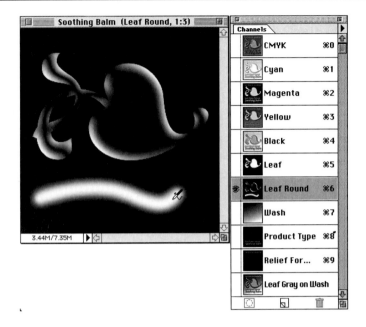

Figure 2.16
A selection can be saved in any channel, replacing the channel's contents, or it can be saved as a new channel.

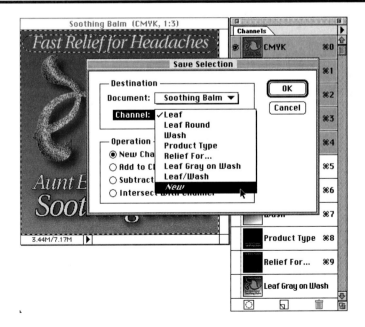

Figure 2.17
Channels can be easily reorganized within the Channels palette for display purposes or for better organization.

Figure 2.18
A comprehensive set of calculation commands allows you to process same-size channels in numerous ways, placing the results of the calculation into any same-size channel or creating a new same-size channel.

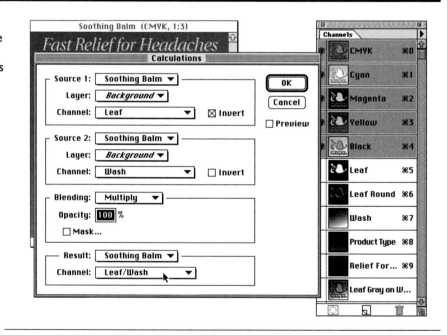

Summary

Here are the key points we've covered in this chapter:

- Traditional masks with hard edges are used to expose the area of an image that is to be changed, and to protect the other image areas.

- Traditional masks that contain tone are used extensively in special effects photography, and are also used for adjustments to photographic color, tone, and detail.

- Photoshop moves traditional masking practices to the computer, making it easier to use both general types of traditional mask.

- Photoshop's selection tools create electronic masks similar in concept and operation to the frisket masks that airbrush artists use. This book borrows this vocabulary, using the term frisket to describe alpha channel masks generated from Photoshop selection.

- A Photoshop selection functions as the currently active mask, controlling all edits.

- In various ways, Photoshop allows you to view, edit, save, and replace the selection as if it were a special channel. We have termed this special channel the selection buffer.

- In Photoshop terminology, a mask is a selection stored in a channel. To activate the mask, you load it as a selection.

- Photoshop alpha channels are the Photoshop system for storing, editing, moving, and applying calculations to masks.

C H A P T E R

3

Basic Calculations, Commands, and Filters

The Photographic Model
Primary Photoshop Masking Tools

ny of Photoshop's editing tools, commands, and functions that work with grayscale images can be used to make and modify masks. This is because, as discussed in Chapter 2, a Photoshop mask is a selection that is saved in an alpha channel, and all channels are grayscale. There are dozens of potentially useful ways to make masks. Which of them should you use? Just how elegant do your masks need to be?

In most cases it's best to keep the mask as simple as possible. Save the subtle work for when you've loaded the mask as a selection. With the help of a well-designed mask, you'll have a great deal of leeway to modify and fine-tune the visual effect as you edit.

Because a mask is only the vehicle for arriving at your desired image, you can usually get by with a few basic calculations, commands, and functions to construct the mask. This chapter discusses these basics. As you gain experience you can add to your list of favorite techniques and turn to additional tools as the need arises. Don't be surprised, however, if the basics turn out to be all you really need.

The Photographic Model

Photographic masks were introduced briefly in Chapter 2, but now it's time to discuss them in greater depth because they form the foundation for Photoshop masking concepts. A good deal of the special effects presented later in this book have been performed by skilled photographic technicians for years. In many cases, work that used to take several hours now takes just a minute or two in Photoshop, but the basic plan for achieving the effects remains the same. These basic photographic techniques should form the core of your

masking know-how, and because you can do so much with them, it's worth learning them well.

The Key Techniques

Much photographic special-effect masking relies on six key techniques: superimposition or multiple exposure, duplication, defocusing, converting between positive and negative, misregistering images with one another, and choking and spreading. Photoshop provides the equivalent of these six key photographic functions in computer form, as listed in Table 3.1.

Table 3.1   **Photographic Masking Techniques and the Matching Photoshop Operations**

Photographic Effect	Photoshop Operation
Superimposition	Multiply
Duplication	Duplicate File or Duplicate Channel
Defocusing	Gaussian Blur
Positive-Negative	Invert
Misregistration	Offset (manual or via filter)
Choking, Spreading	Contract, Expand, Minimum, Maximum

The above photographic techniques offer almost limitless possibilities, depending on how and in what order the various effects are applied. For example, a photographer might sandwich film of an original mask in register with film of a blurred negative of that mask to produce an outglow mask (Figure 3.1).

The above Photoshop operations, plus Photoshop's Difference calculation and Levels command, give you a versatile suite of basic computerized mask-construction tools. Most of the rest of this chapter introduces and demonstrates these tools. Their use in concert is discussed throughout this book.

Figure 3.1
In many photographic masking techniques, you superimpose films. Here, a positive mask of a spade (left) is superimposed in register on a blurred negative copy (center) to produce an outglow mask (right).

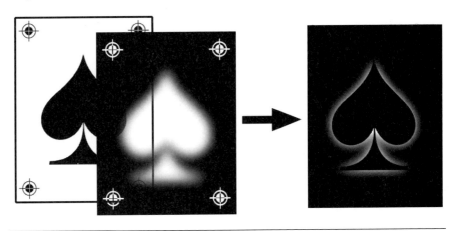

Primary Photoshop Masking Tools

Photoshop masking is like a very simple language. You can learn its basics in a few days, but like all languages, it takes time to develop fluency. Following is the vocabulary for basic Photoshop masking.

Multiply

The Multiply calculation command serves as your "superimposition" tool. Two images multiplied together appear as if superimposed on a light table—dark areas dominate light ones—and detail is preserved in the partially transparent areas (Figure 3.2). The practical utility of the Multiply command cannot be overstated. The other calculation commands have their roles, to be sure, but you should learn to use Multiply first.

Figure 3.2
With Photoshop you can emulate the superimposition of film by multiplying two images together. This allows you to use many well-established photographic masking techniques in Photoshop. For example, an outglow mask similar to the one illustrated in Figure 3.1 can be produced by multiplying a positive mask and a blurred, inverted copy of that mask.

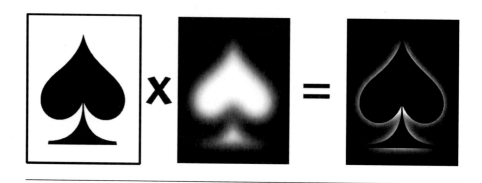

Duplicate File and Duplicate Channel

To make exact copies of files or channels, Photoshop provides the Duplicate File and Duplicate Channel commands. Most masks are built by modifying and combining duplicates of existing channels. Therefore, Duplicate Channel may be the command you use most.

Gaussian Blur

The Gaussian Blur filter is a precise defocusing tool. You control the amount of defocusing with the pixel radius setting, which you can vary by increments of 0.1 pixel. In certain circumstances the Motion Blur or Radial Blur filters can be used instead of the Gaussian Blur filter. As with any Photoshop function that operates with a pixel radius, this filter's effect depends on the resolution of the file to which you apply it (Figure 3.3). With larger pixels, the blurring is spread over a larger region, so the same radius will give you a greater visual blur in a low-resolution image (where the pixels are large) than in a high-resolution one (where the pixels are small).

Figure 3.3
The effect you get with Gaussian Blur depends on the resolution of your image file. With its pixel-based radius setting, blurring is less apparent in a high-resolution file (left) than in a low-resolution file (right).

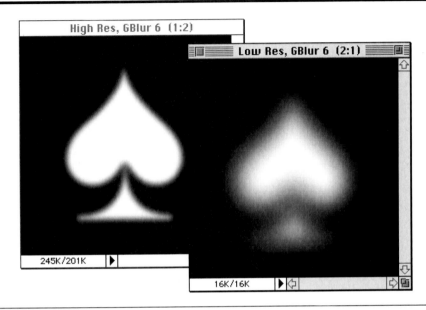

Invert

The Invert command lets you quickly convert a positive image to negative, and vice-versa. This function comes into play so often that Invert shows up as a choice in various dialog boxes, including the Duplicate Channel dialog box.

Offset

To position two channels out of register, you can manually reposition one or both of them by selecting and dragging, a technique that works well when you are viewing both channels simultaneously (Figure 3.4). When the situation calls for it, you can also reposition with numerical accuracy by using the Offset filter. With this filter you move an image by specifying the offset in pixels right and down; to move left or up you use negative numbers (Figure 3.5). In principle you could choose instead to put one or both channels into Layers and position them, but in most cases this would be overkill.

Figure 3.4
The Move tool allows you to position channels manually. Setting their displays to different colors helps you see the positions more easily.

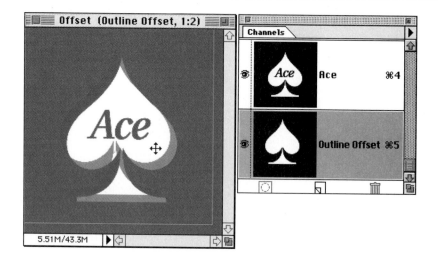

Figure 3.5
The Offset filter allows repositioning with numerical accuracy.

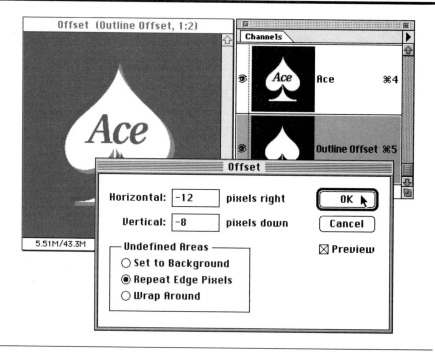

Contract, Expand, Minimum, and Maximum

Choking and spreading are used in small amounts for trapping in color prepress work. When used in large amounts they can serve as creative masking tools. For selections, choking is performed by the Contract command and spreading is performed by the Expand command (Figure 3.6). Essentially the same results can be achieved by applying the Minimum and Maximum filters to masks. With all four of these functions you specify the amount of choke or spread in pixels. Soft edges are preserved. Before applying these commands you must consider the nature of the selection or channel. To obtain the result you want, sometimes you'll need to use Inverse (for selections) or Invert (for channels) before applying the command.

Figure 3.6
The Contract and Expand commands allow you to precisely choke and spread selections. The Minimum and Maximum filters perform the same effect on existing channels. In this case the Contracted and Expanded selections were subsequently saved to channels.

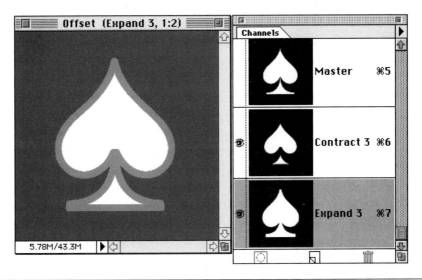

Difference

Only by a complex set of photographic steps would you be able to achieve the results that Photoshop's Difference calculation offers. When Difference is applied to two images, areas where the two images have widely differing brightness levels result in bright pixels. Areas where the levels are close in value—no matter how bright they happen to be—result in dark pixels. Even for experienced users of this command, the results often prove surprising and pleasing (Figure 3.7).

Figure 3.7
Difference calculations can be used to achieve a variety of results. Performing a Difference calculation on two blurred, offset channels, for example, yields a mask that can be used for a roundness or chrome effect.

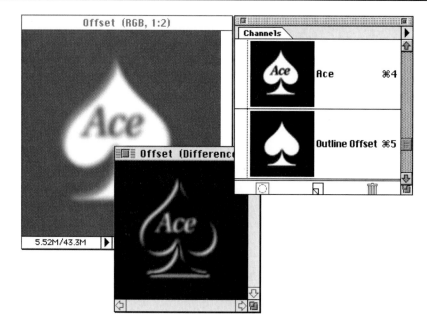

Levels

Very often you need to adjust the tone of a mask. The Levels command works splendidly for this by allowing you to see the distribution of the brightness levels and giving you ample tone control for most mask construction.

Other Actors: Lighter, Add, and Screen

Other calculation commands come in handy, although they are not as indispensable as Duplicate, Multiply, and Difference. The Lighter calculation is useful for combining light material in two channels with dark backgrounds when the lighter regions of the material do not overlap. If the light-on-dark material overlaps and you want to preserve detail, Add is useful—but you need to study the command a bit to learn how to use the scale and offset fields in its dialog box. Screen, the inverse of Multiply, provides useful surprises (although it offers nothing you can't do one way or another with Multiply).

Exclusion of any command from this chapter's list does not mean you should ignore it! These are merely the most frequently used and indispensable commands for basic mask-making. As you gain experience you will work with all of the commands, and you will no doubt develop your own favorites.

Summary

Here are the key points we've covered in this chapter:

- The best masks are often the simplest masks.

- Many of the most interesting Photoshop special-effect masks rely on a small but powerful set of basic operations: Multiply, Duplicate File or Duplicate Channel, Gaussian Blur, Invert, Offset, Contract, Expand, Minimum, and Maximum.

- Used in concert, these calculations, commands, and filters can generate an enormous variety of masks and effects, as discussed throughout this book.

- In addition to these features, the Difference, Lighter, Add, and Screen calculations, and the Levels command, figure among the most powerful Photoshop mask construction tools.

CHAPTER

4

Layers

dobe Photoshop 3.0 introduced Layers, a feature that allows you to superimpose elements of an image "as if they were on sheets of clear acetate." Actually, the sheets-of-acetate metaphor does not do justice to the power and flexibility of this feature, because with Layers you can do much more than just superimpose elements. For starters, you can blend the elements in numerous ways, adjust any layer's transparency with a mask, and use layers as transparency masks for one another.

Floating selections have been available in Photoshop for a long time. These individual temporary layers gave a hint of what was to come. In providing numerous full-fledged layers, Photoshop's creative universe has expanded to the point where no two people on the planet are likely to approach this software in the same way. This book's procedures do not rely on layers, but you can use them with layers as your working style evolves.

A powerful creative tool requires time to absorb. As this book is written, few people have had the opportunity to work extensively with Photoshop layers. This chapter discusses concepts and practices that are evident now, with the awareness that time and experience may offer additional insights on this subject.

This chapter assumes you are familiar with the basic Layers information presented in the Adobe Photoshop 3.0 User Guide, which this book often calls the Photoshop manual. This chapter covers some of the more advanced Layers concepts. As a result, the level of the discussion goes a bit beyond that of the previous three chapters. For some readers, it will therefore be helpful to skip over the more technical sections of this chapter and jump right into Chapter 5 to start generating drop shadows and glows. Some hands-on experience with masks will help you take full advantage of the advanced Layers features discussed in this chapter.

Layers Concepts

In effect, each Photoshop layer is an additional color image that can have transparent, partly transparent, and opaque regions. A layer blends with the layers and background beneath it according to the same modes—Normal, Lighter, Darker, Multiply, and so on—that are used for the painting and editing tools. You can set a layer's opacity in 1 percent increments from 0 percent to 100 percent (Figure 4.1). You can also vary the opacity in other, more complex ways that are discussed later in this chapter. In theory you can add up to 99 layers to a document, but practical considerations are likely to limit you to one or two dozen, depending on the needs of your image and the amount of RAM you have available.

Figure 4.1

This image consists of a blue wash background plus a single layer that contains the gray sphere and its drop shadow. The Layer Options dialog box offers precise control of blending, including the full range of modes; you select these modes via the pop-up menu. In this case the blending is as simple as possible: 100 percent Opacity, Normal mode, no slider adjustments, and no grouping.

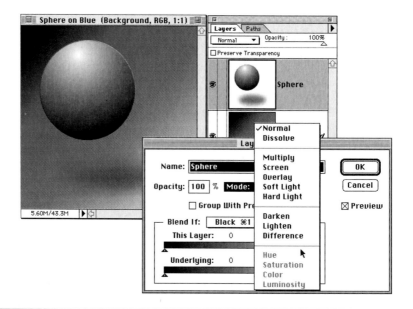

In addition to the Layers basics you can pick up from the Photoshop manual and from casual experimentation, the Layers user should master the following three areas:

- Using the blending sliders
- Manipulating opacity
- Using layers wisely

The following sections discuss these topics in detail.

The Blending Sliders

In Photoshop 2.5.1, the Composite Controls dialog box lets you control the way a floating selection blends with the image beneath it. Photoshop 3.0 relies on the same mechanism but packages it into the Layer Options dialog box. The blending modes, grouping, and opacity choices are also conveniently duplicated in the Layers palette, where most users prefer to access them. Few users of Photoshop 2.5.1 mastered the Composite Control sliders, but advanced work with layers makes this step necessary and invaluable.

Remember that image data consists of brightness values and pixel addresses. Photoshop puts these brightness values to work when you use the blending sliders. Before Photoshop can blend pixels, it needs to know which pixels to blend and in what proportions to blend them. By default it blends all pixels in a layer with all the pixels that underlie that layer. By using pixel brightness values to determine which pixels will be blended, Photoshop opens up a host of new possibilities that can help you quickly achieve effects that would otherwise require laborious mask construction.

The active layer's pixels are always the ones that are sacrificed when you move the sliders. To learn how to manipulate the sliders, it's best to begin with a simple image. Figures 4.2 and 4.3 show the slider system in action, with various color-coded arrows to indicate the regions affected by the sliders. To make the effects as clear as possible, the layer to be blended contains just a full range of gray brightness levels (all tones from black to white), and the background consists of a simple blue wash, again with a wide range of brightness values.

The This Layer Sliders

In Figure 4.2, by moving the positions of the This Layer sliders (using the Option key to split them), five different pixel-brightness regions can be established. Moving from left to right along the slider, first the layer pixels with brightness levels below 12 are completely eliminated from blending—the black drop shadow and the darkest edge of the sphere no longer appear in the image. Next, the shadow slider is split from level 12 to level 48, feathering the shadow pixels at the bottom of the sphere and allowing the blue background to partially show through. In the middle zone between level 48 and level 184, the sphere blends with full opacity. Next, the highlight slider is split from level 184 to level 233, feathering the highlight pixels at the top of the sphere and again allowing the background to partially show through. Finally, the right half of the highlight slider eliminates the

Figure 4.2
The This Layer slider uses brightness levels to determine which layer pixels will appear in the blend. The color-coded arrows show the regions of the gray sphere layer affected by the colored areas of the slider. See text for details.

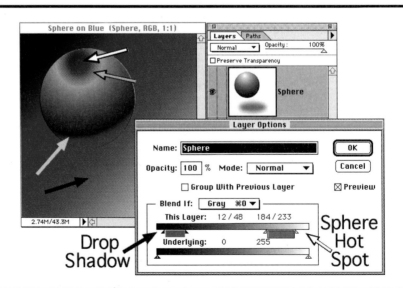

pixels above level 233 from blending, so the background completely shows through the pixels in the sphere's hot spot.

The Underlying Sliders

In Figure 4.3 the This Layer sliders are returned to the 0 and 255 positions, and the Underlying shadow sliders are moved without splitting them. Now the underlying pixels with brightness levels below 38 and above 112 are completely eliminated from blending— but in this case they replace active layer pixels (again, active layer pixels are always sacrificed by slider adjustments). The unblended underlying pixels now appear completely in the image. The ragged edges near the heads of the arrows are caused by variations in pixel brightness level that occur when the Gradient tool's dithering option is used. Dithering reduces tonal banding, and was in effect when I first created the sphere and drop shadow.

Figure 4.3
The Underlying slider also uses brightness levels to determine which layer pixels will appear in the blend. In this illustration, underlying pixels whose brightness is below 38 (pink arrow) and above 112 (green arrow) replace active layer pixels completely. See text for details.

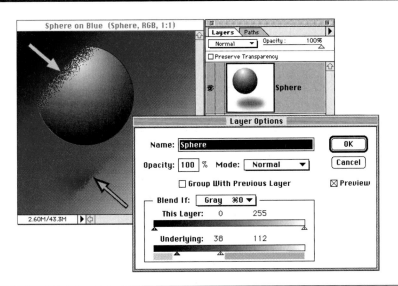

NOTE: *The blending sliders can use the brightness levels in individual color channels available in the pop-up menu. Experiment with the effects on highly colored material.*

Subtle Effects

It's one thing to see the blending sliders in action on an analytical image like the one in Figures 4.1 to 4.3. In practical use the sliders can help you create pleasing subtle blends such as those shown in Figures 4.4 to 4.7.

Figure 4.4
In a multilayer image, the leaf layer blocks out all other material when blended at 100 percent opacity in Normal mode.

Figure 4.5
Splitting the This Layer shadow slider eliminates most of the black surrounding the leaf.

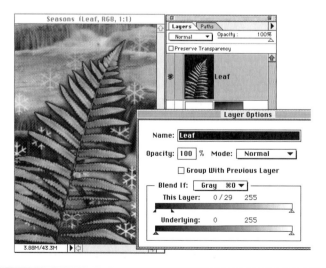

Figure 4.6
Making additional adjustments allows the underlying pixels to show through, giving the leaf a brightness-based transparent feeling that would not be possible with a simple opacity adjustment.

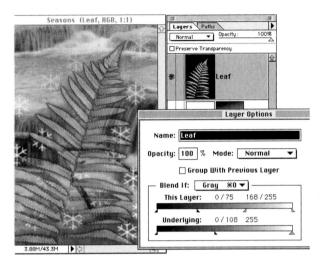

Figure 4.7
The completed image with its Layers palette

Opacity

In order to have layers appear as if they are on clear sheets of acetate with all the adjustments that users want, Photoshop has four major mechanisms that manage layer transparency. These are the layer's overall opacity setting, the blending sliders, and two specialized masks. The layer's overall opacity setting and the blending sliders have already been discussed in the previous sections. The Transparency mask, while always in effect, can only be seen indirectly— through the Apply Image or Calculations dialog boxes with Preview toggled on, or by using Apply Image, Calculations, or Load Selection/ Save as a Selection to copy it to an alpha channel as in Figure 4.8. The Layer mask appears in the Layers palette. It also appears in the Channel palette when the layer to which it's attached is active.

Figure 4.8
The Sphere layer's Layer mask appears next to the layer thumbnail. Because the layer is active, the mask also appears in the Channels palette. The Sphere layer's Transparency mask, captured as a saved selection and visible at the bottom of the Channels palette, defines the transparent regions of the layer. This saved selection can be edited, but the Transparency mask itself is not directly editable.

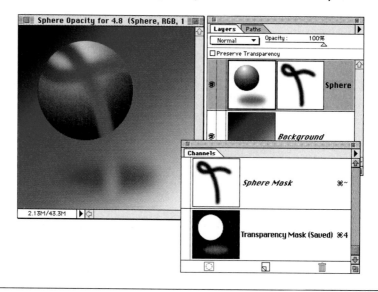

Note that Photoshop uses the term *transparency* in some places and *opacity* in others, referring to essentially the same characteristic. The key difference is that opacity and transparency are the inverse of one another—if a layer has an opacity of 60 percent it is 40 percent transparent, and so forth.

The Transparency Mask

The Transparency mask is lighter in areas where a layer is more opaque. When the Preserve Transparency box is checked in the Layers palette, edits to the active layer occur through the Transparency mask as if it were an "opacity selection." In this state, regions of the layer previously defined as transparent cannot be affected. If you also happen to have a regular selection active while editing with Preserve Transparency checked, the Transparency mask and the selection work together; edits occur only in regions that are selected by both (Figure 4.9).

Figure 4.9
When the Preserve Transparency option is checked in the Layers palette, both the Layer mask and the Transparency mask control edits. In this case, both masks also control any selection that may be active.

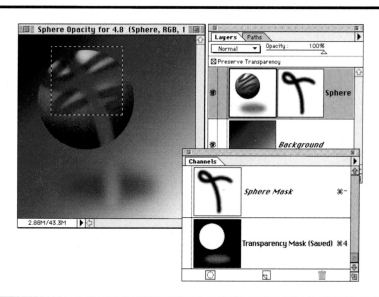

When you apply the Group command to one or more layers, the Transparency mask for the bottom layer in the group (the *base layer*) is applied to the entire group (Figure 4.10). The Photoshop manual calls such a group a *clipping group*, which, if you use the PostScript clipping-path concept, implies a hard outline. In fact, the Transparency mask has no such restrictions. It is a Photoshop mask and has all the capacity for edge softness and tonal detail that this implies (Figure 4.11).

Figure 4.10
In a layers clipping group, the base layer's Transparency mask controls the entire group. In this case the base layer's object has a hard outline.

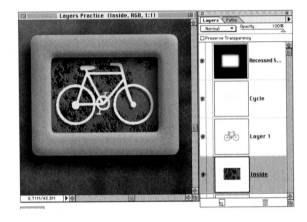

Figure 4.11
Transparency masks are contone masks, so the clipping can be hard, soft, or partly transparent. Here, the layer with the soft-edged drop shadow acts as the base layer, and the clipping that results is soft.

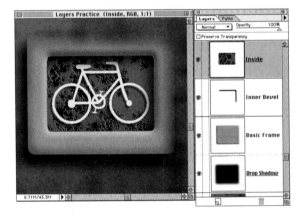

You have no direct way to edit the Transparency mask, but you can use it in the following situations:

- To select the contents of a layer, press Command+Option+T to load the Transparency mask as a selection. You can then use this selection to control your edit or you can save it to an alpha channel—a neat way to "capture" the Transparency mask.

- Using the Calculations command, you can save the Transparency mask directly to an alpha channel or you can employ it in channel calculations.

An interesting thing happens when you use the painting tools with an opacity setting of less than 100 percent. The tool applies color at full strength—but also writes to the Transparency mask, reducing the visible effect according to the tool's opacity setting. When you later perform operations that check a pixel's brightness values, they don't see the Transparency mask; they respond as if the original edit had been performed at 100 percent opacity. For example, notice how, in response to the change in the blending sliders, the drop shadow in the illustration used for Figures 4.1–4.3 has vanished in Figure 4.2, along with other material that is completely black. This happens because the original drop shadow was painted with black, not gray. The drop shadow only appears dark gray because the Transparency mask reduces the black to an opacity of about 30 percent.

Layer Masks

The place for directly editing a layer's transparency is the Layer mask. In Figure 4.8, with default settings, the Layer mask is darker in areas where the layer is more transparent and lighter in areas where the layer is more opaque, the same convention used by the Transparency mask.

Don't miss the opportunity to view the Layer mask as you edit it by Option-Clicking on the Layer mask's thumbnail in the Layers palette. You can also temporarily inactivate the Layer mask by Command-Clicking on its thumbnail, and you can view the Layer mask in color on the image, channel-display style, by Shift-Clicking on its thumbnail.

Using Layers Wisely

Obviously layers offer many strengths in proper circumstances. Layer-based experimentation and "reactive creativity" can stimulate anyone to produce better images. You should especially consider using layers for

- Creative image development

- Fine-tuning an image's composition, balance, and effects

- Cases where a client might request fast adjustments

- Preparing variations on an image

- Duplicating a section of a layer for seamless fixes

All of these situations can lead you to fill an image file with layers as you try variations (Figure 4.12 and 4.13), or to perform spot fixes (Figure 4.14). As noted in the next section, having many layers can force some trade-offs.

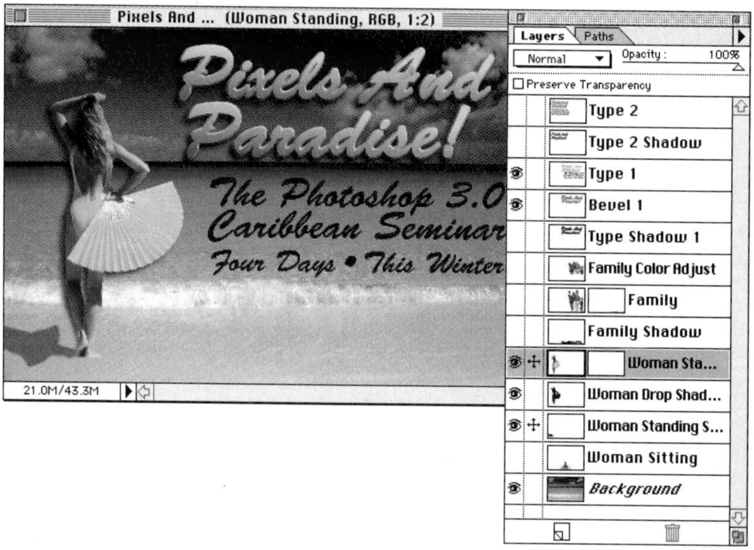

Figure 4.12
If you have the RAM (and the patience) you can fill an image with layers to examine variations.

Figure 4.13
Switching a
few layers can
allow you to
cover all your
conceptual
bases!

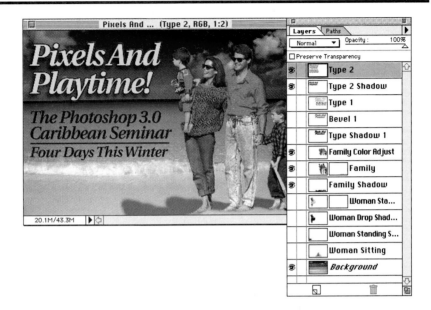

Figure 4.14
You can also use
layers for spot
corrections to
offer ready
comparisons. The
inset shows the
area of the
"Family Color
Adjust" layer
with the layer
visible.

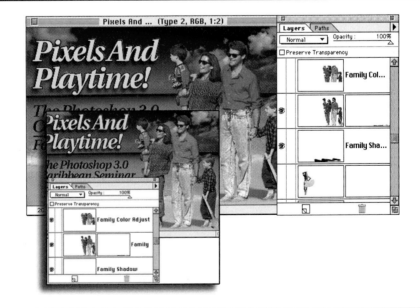

The Potential Disadvantages

Because each layer is an additional color image, it places significant demands on your computer system. If your image is moderately large in size and moderately high in resolution, adding numerous layers can quickly exhaust the RAM assigned to Photoshop. In response, the program begins to use your hard disk to handle the overflow, which slows down performance and increases the time it takes you to finish your work.

Also, working with layers requires a certain amount of mouse activity, which can sometimes be avoided by using simpler methods. Layers are so intuitive that you might find yourself using them for routine jobs when the same result can be achieved faster with a few simple keystrokes and a few mouse clicks.

The point of diminishing returns with layers depends on how you work and what you need to accomplish, so it's not possible to give hard-and-fast rules. The best advice is this: Think before you automatically work with multiple layers, merge layers whenever you can (Figure 4.15), and use layers as sparingly as possible.

Figure 4.15
The layers for each concept in Figures 4.12 and 4.13 have been merged. The document now uses less memory.

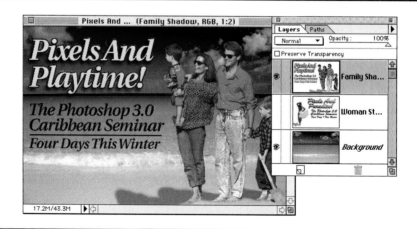

Here are a few situations where layers should probably be used sparingly or not at all:

- When you are making minor adjustments to existing images (work on a copy instead)

- When you can quickly get the same result in other ways (simple drop shadows, simple glow effects, and so forth)

- When you plan to change color mode repeatedly (changing modes flattens layers)

- When your image's file size is large and your RAM is limited

- Whenever you can't use a Photoshop 3.0 file in the next step (Photoshop 3.0 is the only file format that recognizes layers)

When using several layers, it makes sense to continuously check your RAM usage by monitoring Scratch Sizes at the lower-left corner of your document window.

When the number on the left (the current memory usage) exceeds the number on the right (available RAM), Photoshop will begin using your hard disk for scratch files. When this occurs, it's time to close files, merge layers, or resign yourself to taking a bit longer to work.

Masks and Layers

You might hear that using layers makes it unnecessary to use masks with Photoshop 3.0. This is incorrect. For most of the effects presented in this book, masks are still essential. It is true, though, that layers reduce the need for certain types of basic knockout masks for simple drop shadows and glows. These masks are presented in this book because their principles still come into play. In particular, using knockout masks can teach you some handy techniques.

Often, taking the mask approach can save you time—even if you don't use the masks directly. For example, in a case where you need a simple drop shadow or simple glow, you can use a simple set of steps to build a selection that gives you just what you need, without saving more than one channel and without using a single extra layer. For details on this technique, see Chapter 8, Figure 8.7. With practice, techniques like this can take much less time than building the effect in layers, and they use less RAM.

As always, the guiding rule should be common sense. If it makes sense to use the enormous power of layers, by all means do! When it's wiser to use other means, that's the way to go.

Summary

Here are the key points we've covered in this chapter:

- In effect, each layer is a separate color image that can have transparent and opaque regions.

- Each layer blends with the material below it according to the settings you make.

- To make the best use the enormous creative power of layers, you need to learn how to work with opacity.

- Opacity is affected by the opacity slider, the blending sliders, the Layer mask, and the Transparency mask.

- The blending sliders, the Transparency mask, and the layer mask, all require some practice, but this practice pays off by giving you greater access to the power of Layers.

- Using numerous layers can require a substantial amount of RAM, possibly forcing Photoshop to use your hard disk for scratch files and slowing your work. To minimize this, it's advisable to use layers where they can do you the most good, and to manage layers carefully.

- For simple effects, basic strategies can often produce results that are as good as you could obtain from layers but only take a fraction of the time.

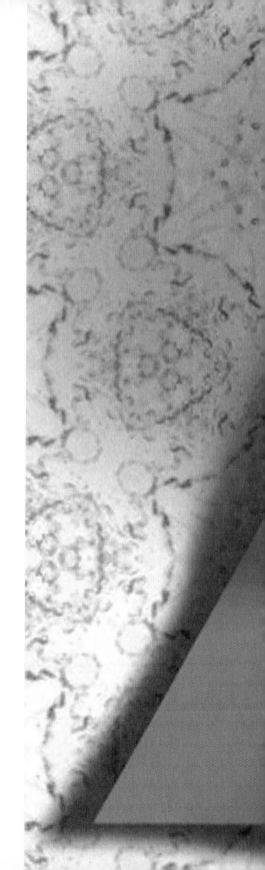

2

Making and Using Masks

CHAPTER

5

Making a Set of Frisket Masks

Experimenting

A Set of Basic Masks

Metallic Background Showing through Cutout in Textured Foreground

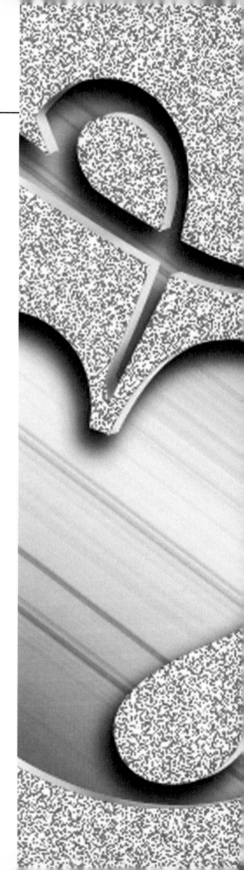

This chapter presents ways to construct some simple frisket masks and two images, using the concepts discussed. Later chapters refer back to some of the steps presented here.

You can't just read the following exercises. You need to perform them in Photoshop as you go, because this is one situation where it is definitely easier to do than to tell! A simple 10-second procedure can take a complex paragraph to describe—but run through it in Photoshop twice and it's easy.

These masks and images could be built in many ways. The procedures offered here are orderly and easy to follow. You'll have plenty of time to develop your own clever mask-building methods once you get some practice.

As noted in Chapter 4, a simple mask often works as well or better than an elegant one, and a simple mask takes less time to build. Keep your masks simple. Add complexity later, as you edit the image through the mask.

Experimenting

Once a mask is built, you can use it to make many variations on an image. You should reproduce the masks described in this chapter and create different images with them. Then build and experiment with other masks of your own.

Purposeful experimentation in Photoshop will help you find many useful ways to accomplish interesting effects. While you experiment, keep track of what you are doing so you can retrace, refine, and simplify the paths to the many cool effects you'll discover.

As you work through the following procedures, save your intermediate images every now and then. This way, if an experiment goes awry you won't have to start all over from scratch.

A Set of Basic Masks

We'll use a set of basic masks to make a simple image, in this case a flat, metallic letterform floating slightly above a textured background. All lighting effects in this chapter are generated with the masks and edits, not with Photoshop's lighting filters. The lighting and position cues in this image come from a simple drop shadow. A diffuse light source appears to be placed to the upper right, out of the frame of the image.

Create a new RGB file named *Friskets 1*, add a new alpha channel, and choose a color and opacity for the new channel's display in the Channel Options dialog box (Figure 5.1). Name the new channel *Master*. Since you're just practicing, the file's resolution isn't critical, but lower resolutions have fewer pixels for the computer to crunch, so they'll process faster.

Figure 5.1
The Channel Options dialog box lets you determine how a channel will be displayed when you view it with other channels.

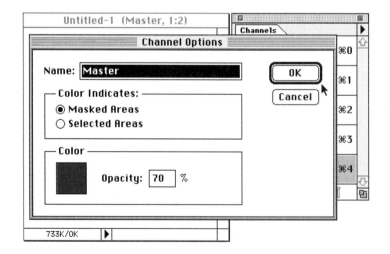

A Simple Frisket Mask

Now you can make a simple frisket mask by placing a type object in the Master channel. View both the Master channel and the RGB image as you position the type in the channel—click in the leftmost column of the Channels palette to display the alpha channel as if it were an overlay placed over the color composite channel. (I like to work with a white channel background as illustrated in the figures, so before I placed the type I changed the channel background from black to white.)

Now place an anti-aliased dingbat in a large point size in the new Master channel. (I used a Zapf Dingbat Option+7.) You'll see the dingbat in the Master channel superimposed over the RGB image, which is still white at this stage. The Master channel is displayed with the color and opacity you chose earlier in this example.

Position and drop the dingbat where you like (Figure 5.2). The Master channel now contains a simple frisket mask with the dingbat shape in black on a white background. (Note: These instructions assume that you have installed the necessary fonts and Adobe Type Manager. If your computer refuses to create very large type characters, or if they come up bitmapped, try increasing the Font Cache size for Adobe Type Manager or check your Photoshop documentation.)

Figure 5.2
Place the dingbat in a channel while viewing the channel superimposed on the image (in this case the RGB image is all white). This allows you to position the dingbat freely as you make a mask for later use.

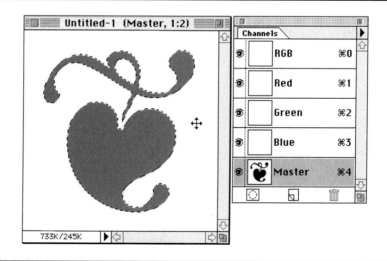

To actually experiment with the frisket mask, load Master as the selection, working in the RGB composite view. Depending on how you have set up your copy of Photoshop, the selection will appear in one of two ways: Either the dingbat shape will be selected or the area around the shape will be selected. It's easy to change back and forth between these two situations: The Inverse command reverses the "polarity" of the selection. Practice filling the selected region (the dingbat) with various colors, patterns, and textures. You can hide the marquee as you work with Command+H. Then change the polarity of the selection with Inverse and keep experimenting on the background around the dingbat.

In my case, I filled the dingbat with a brushed aluminum texture using a standard preset available in the Gradient Designer module of Kai's Power Tools. I then inverted the selection, applied mono-chromatic noise, and colorized to a red using the Colorize feature of the Hue/Saturation command (Figure 5.3).

Figure 5.3
By using the Inverse command, you can make the frisket mask named Master serve for editing both the dingbat and its background. Here the dingbat contains a brushed aluminum texture from Kai's Power Tools. The background is a colorized noise texture.

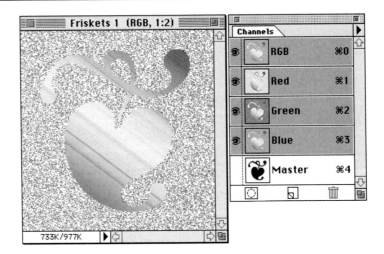

A Drop-Shadow Mask

There are several quick-and-dirty Photoshop tricks for making drop shadows. With many of them you create a drop shadow on the color image before it is complete, so it's hard to fine-tune the shadow later. A mask allows you to fine-tune the drop shadow once the rest of the image is in place.

Duplicate the Master channel, name the new channel *GBlur 6*, and assign it a display color different from the display color of Master. Apply a Gaussian Blur of radius 6 to channel GBlur 6. Invert GBlur 6 and offset it down and to the left from the Master channel (Figure 5.4). I did the offset manually with the Move tool so I could watch the effect while displaying the Master and GBlur 6 channels together. To avoid leaving white gaps in the channel, I set Photoshop's background color to black for the move step. Offsetting down and to the left places the shadow properly for a light source high and to the right.

Figure 5.4
Viewing two channels at once, you can manually adjust the offset of the GBlur 6 channel by selecting and dragging it. Note the different channel display colors.

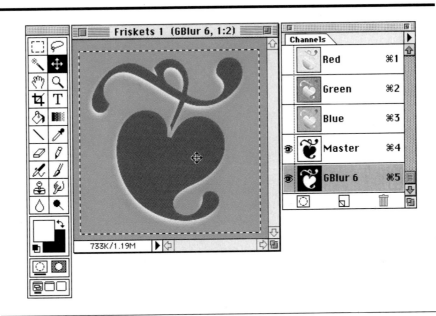

Now Multiply the GBlur 6 channel by the Master channel and place the result of this calculation in a new channel. To do this, use the Calculations command, which brings up a big dialog box full of pop-up menus. In the dialog box specify Source 1 to be file *Friskets 1*, channel *Master*; Source 2 to be file *Friskets 1*, channel *GBlur 6*; Blending as *Multiply*; Opacity as *100 percent*; and place the result in file *Friskets 1* as a new channel. Name the new channel *Drop Shadow*.

When you multiply, the dark regions of the Master channel knock the dingbat shape out of the light areas of the GBlur 6 channel, leaving just the shadow area, which Photoshop places in the Drop Shadow channel (Figure 5.5). Save Friskets 1 at this point—you'll probably want to try various experiments starting with the image as it now stands. The Photoshop 2.5 and Photoshop 3.0 formats save alpha-channel masks very efficiently.

Figure 5.5
Multiplying the Master and GBlur 6 channels knocks the Master's outline out of GBlur 6 to give the Drop Shadow mask.

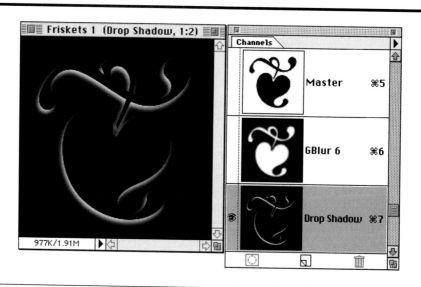

With the advent of Layers, drop-shadow masks of this type aren't nearly as critical for work in Photoshop 3.0 as they used to be for work in Photoshop 2.5.1, but it is important to know how to make them and use them. The steps used above form the basis for masks that are more complex—and which you'll use often in Photoshop 3.0.

Drop Shadows and Color Modes

In cases where an image is to be printed, you must consider which ink will carry the drop shadow. Synthetic drop shadows can cause trouble when printed, because you usually want the shadow to be a dark neutral gray. If you simply darken a drop-shadow area in an RGB file and later separate this file to CMYK, all four process inks participate in printing the shadow. This makes the shadow quite sensitive to minor inking variations on the press. The shadow can develop a distracting color cast if the ink balance changes slightly, a common occurrance. To avoid this problem, most prepress shops recommend that you make the drop shadow with black ink only by placing the shadow in the black channel of a CMYK file.

So before applying the drop shadow, change the mode from RGB to CMYK via the Mode menu. (Changing color mode is not a trivial matter. Your Monitor Setup, Printing Inks Setup, and Separation Setup Preferences settings control the way CMYK channels are generated from an RGB file. This is a subject outside the scope of this book. Check the Adobe manual for information. For the purposes of this particular exercise, the Preferences settings aren't critical.)

Once the RGB-to-CMYK mode change is complete, arrange to write information to the Black channel only: In the Channels palette, click on the Black channel, then click again in the left column in the CMYK composite channel. This way you can view the whole image, including the drop shadow, in color while writing just to the Black channel (Figure 5.6).

Figure 5.6
The file is now CMYK, the masks are in place, and although all channels are being viewed, the edit will occur in the Black channel only.

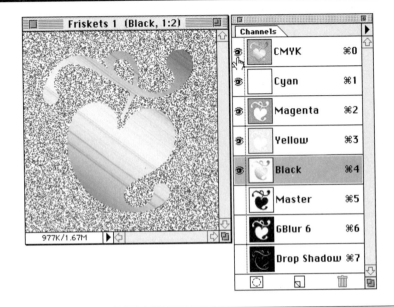

Applying the Drop Shadow

Now that the CMYK file is poised to receive the edit, the drop-shadow application seems almost anticlimactic. As usual in Photoshop, there are several ways to produce a drop shadow with the Drop Shadow mask. Anything that darkens the selected region can be used. In this example, use Levels:

1. Load the Drop Shadow mask and type Command+H to hide the marquee's marching ants.

2. Bring up the Levels dialog box and replace *255* with *40* in the right Output Levels text field, or drag the white triangle at the right end of the Output Levels slider to accomplish the same thing, and click on OK. The result should look like Figure 5.7.

Undo this Levels edit and experiment for a while with different treatments of the drop shadow, working on all channels as well as just the Black channel. On this particular image, the Levels command

Figure 5.7
The appearance of the image after the Master mask is loaded and Levels is used to darken the drop-shadow region.

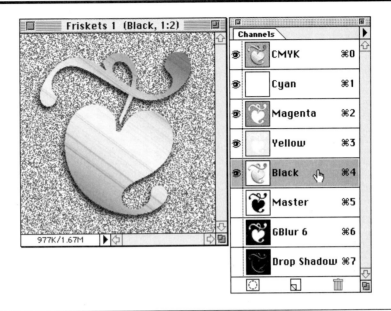

doesn't have much to work with, but on other images it works very well (try adjusting the Input Levels sliders as well as the Output Levels sliders). On different images try filling with various percentages of black, change hue slightly and darken with Hue/Saturation, and so forth.

Drop-Shadow Variations

You can produce a wide variety of drop shadows by varying the amount of blurring, amount of offset, and direction of offset as you build drop-shadow masks. Increasing the blur softens the shadow, indicating a more diffuse light source and a greater separation between the shadow-casting object and the background. Varying the amount and direction of offset casts the shadow in different directions, which gives cues about the relative positions of the light source, the shadow-casting object, and the background.

Metallic Background Showing through Cutout in Textured Foreground

Once you have a set of mask intermediates, you can often combine them in different ways to produce various different effects. In this example, the Master and GBlur 6 channels easily produce a drop shadow of another interesting variety: a *Recessed-Shadow mask.* Starting back with the Friskets 1 RGB file, Invert both Master and GBlur 6. This reverses the dark and light areas in both channels. Now multiply Master and GBlur 6, place the result in a new channel, and name this new channel *Recessed Shadow* (Figure 5.8).

Figure 5.8
When you invert the Master and GBlur 6 channels and multiply them together, a recessed-shadow mask results.

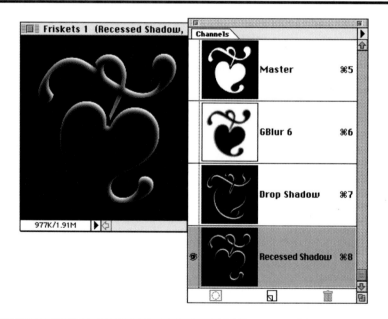

Apply the above Levels treatment, using the recessed drop shadow instead of the standard drop shadow, to get the effect shown in Figure 5.9.

Figure 5.9
The same Levels drop-shadow edit from Figure 5.7, applied this time using the recessed-shadow mask

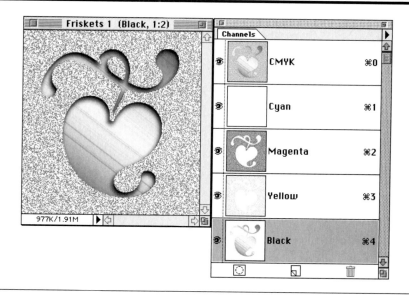

For a nice finishing touch, build an inside bevel mask (see Chapter 10), fill it with white or light gray, and perhaps airbrush in a few subtle shadows (Figure 5.10).

Figure 5.10
With an inside bevel mask and airbrushing (see Chapter 10) you can give the impression of a textured foreground, die-cut to reveal a chrome layer underneath.

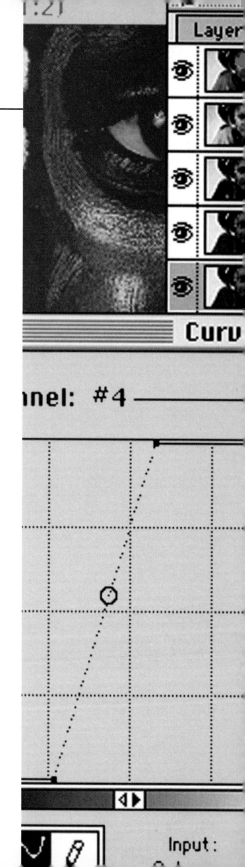

CHAPTER

Making Masks from Existing Images

Make a Plan

The Four Basic Approaches

*Making a Frisket Mask to Silhouette
a Photo*

hapter 5 discussed how to make complex masks starting with simple frisket masks. When you make simple frisket masks before using them to generate the image, you can finesse the mask edges to your taste. However, when you must isolate portions of an existing image for editing, it is the content of the image that determines the edges of the resulting selection or mask.

When the edge of a mask or selection isn't right, the seams of your edit may show against the rest of the image. To avoid this problem you may find yourself spending hours making careful selections and checking the results. Because that approach is not an economical way to spend your time, this chapter is designed to help you make frisket masks faster—and with better edges, too.

Make a Plan

Tip A small image to be printed with a coarse halftone screen may not require much fiddling with the masks, because these images can often tolerate two or three pixels of error in the mask edges. For large images or images intended for high-quality printing, you'll need to be more careful.

Whatever the situation, always pause for a few moments to think about the mask you need. Don't begin until you've decided exactly what you need to do. Then make a plan for how to use the fewest possible steps to create the mask. If a simple mask can do the job well enough for the image at hand, go for it!

It's rarely a one-click job to make a high-quality mask from the pixels available in a photographic image. Even with the proper selection tools and commands, you should try various settings and evaluate the outcome. Photoshop's selection tools and commands give excellent results in many situations, but there are cases where other methods take less time and deliver better effects.

The Four Basic Approaches

There are four basic approaches you can take to build a mask. Each subsequent approach is more complex as well as more flexible than the preceding ones. The approach you choose depends on the existing image and the mask you need to enhance it. To illustrate each method, we'll use a synthetic image that presents a variety of selection challenges (Figure 6.1).

Figure 6.1
This synthetic image offers a variety of selection and mask challenges. Avoid the temptation to use the Lasso or Pen tools, except as a last resort.

Approach #1: The Lasso and Pen Tools

You can always select regions by brute force, using the Lasso or Pen selection tools. This approach is usually best in circumstances where other tools can't do the job.

Using the Lasso and Pen tools soaks up time! Because their function is so obvious, many people turn to these tools as a first choice. They are appropriate when you have just a moment's work to do, but otherwise use these tools as a last resort—let your computer do the work of selection when possible. Keep the Lasso and Pen in reserve for situations where they alone can do the job you need. Use the

Lasso to touch up small areas that the more automated tools can't handle well, or use the Pen tool to trace the edges of shapes that can't be selected well by other means.

Approach #2: The Magic Wand, Grow, and Similar

You can select regions based on pixel brightnesses or color using the Magic Wand, Grow, or Similar. This approach is appropriate for regions that are well defined by color or tone and that have consistent, easy-to-find boundaries (Figure 6.2).

Figure 6.2
In an area of consistent color with a consistent edge, the Magic Wand easily makes an accurate selection mask. Vary the Tolerance setting as needed.

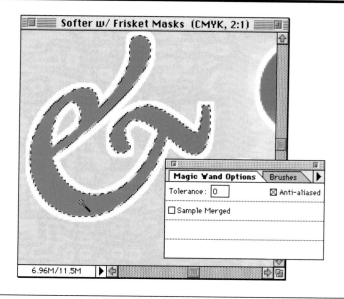

Be ready to change the Magic Wand Tolerance setting often as you work. Try different tolerances until the Magic Wand gives you the selection you need or a selection that is just a little smaller than needed. Then, if necessary, you can reduce the tolerance and apply Grow.

The Pitfalls of Anti-Aliasing and Feathering

The Lasso, Pen, and Magic Wand give you access to automatic anti-aliasing and feathering. Assuming your settings are appropriate, these automated edge treatments work well at the edges of active selections for simple cut-and-paste editing operations. However, they can cause trouble when you perform more complex operations.

To see one example of the problem, try this:

1. Create a scratch image with a simple white background, and set the Lasso tool to use anti-aliasing.

2. Select a region and leave the selection nonfloating.

3. Fill the selection with a dark color, then hit Delete (which fills the selection with the background color).

You will see a telltale ring where the anti-aliased edge of the selection suppresses both the fill and delete operations (unfortunately not in equal amounts). The same holds for feathered selections (Figure 6.3). You can often avoid this problem by floating these kinds of selections before performing operations with them, but if you have saved the selections to use in mask construction, the soft edge pixels can become visible in the future operations.

Figure 6.3
After a fill-and-delete operation, anti-aliasing (upper left) and feathering (lower right) left rings on the image. Soft-edged selections can cause problems if you apply more than a single operation as you edit.

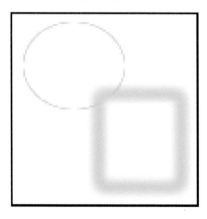

Any time you build a complex mask with calculations using original material that has been anti-aliased or feathered, always examine the mask for telltale "threads" or rings before you use it. It's easier to repair the mask than it is to repair the image later.

Approach #3: Color Range

When the region you want is clearly defined by a particular color, you can select it with Color Range, varying the Fuzziness setting to accommodate complex edges. Color Range offers you several ways to define the range you desire; sampling offers the most flexibility. As you increase fuzziness you expand the range and partially select the pixels that fall in the expanded region (Figure 6.4). Selections made with Color Range should be carefully evaluated: View the selection in Quick Mask mode, as described next.

Figure 6.4
With Color Range, by sampling colors carefully and adjusting Fuzziness you can usually select much or all of the colored region you require. In this particular example, the Lasso (with antialiasing) could then be used to select the remaining region of the S.

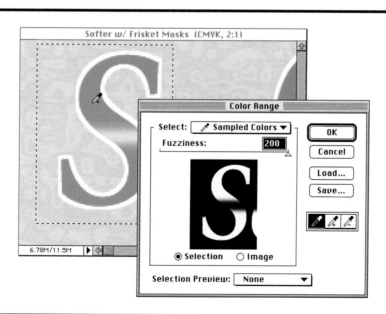

Reviewing with Quick Mask

Working with any of the three above approaches, you'll often use more than one tool as you build a selection. As you work, you can move in and out of Quick Mask mode to see how the edges of the selection mesh with the rest of the image (Figure 6.5).

Figure 6.5
Regardless of which selection tools you use, you can view both your progress and the selection edge by switching into Quick Mask mode, then switching back to Standard mode and continuing with your selection. Most users find it desirable to set a contrasting display color for Quick Mask.

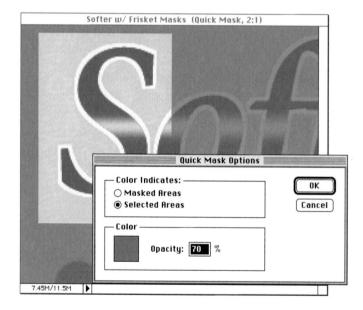

Modifying Detailed Regions

The soft dots with increasingly varied edges in the "Softer & Softer" image pose a problem. It takes several time-consuming steps to construct a good mask for such an image using the simple selection tools. Here's what would be involved:

- Selecting a dot with the Magic Wand
- Applying Similar, and then feathering by a certain amount
- Saving the selection in an alpha channel

- Checking to see which dots the feathered edge would work with

- Repeating the process with different amounts of feathering

- Combining various alpha channels into a single mask

If you become impatient and use a mask with just a single feather value, you can leave obvious flaws after an edit, as in the top row of dots in Figure 6.6.

Figure 6.6
To make a mask for an image with varied edges demands extra time when you use the tolerance-based selection tools. If you work hastily your results may be unsatisfactory, as shown in the top row of dots. In such cases a mask made with Color Range often gives better results, as shown in the bottom row.

The Color Range selection tool can quickly produce a detailed mask to modify the soft dots more accurately, as in the bottom row of dots in Figure 6.6. The mask combines both frisket and contone character (Figure 6.7). When using a mask with soft edges, your edits should be moderate, as discussed below.

Figure 6.7
For regions well defined by color, the Color Range command can quickly produce an accurate, highly detailed mask. This mask was used for the bottom row of dots in Figure 6.6.

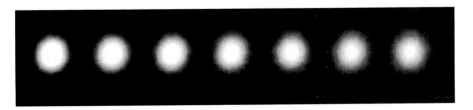

Approach #4: The Power-User Option

As the fourth and most flexible approach, you bypass the selection tools entirely and choose a color channel that has some characteristics of the mask you want. You then duplicate this channel and make a mask of it by modifying it with the tone commands Levels, Curves, and possibly other commands, functions, or filters. This approach requires experience with the Photoshop tone tools. It was the only reasonably fast way to make many kinds of masks until the Color Range command became available in Photoshop 3.0.

This approach can work well with difficult-to-select regions that contain subtle tones or lots of detail. The key is to find a color channel that distinguishes these kinds of areas tonally. Working with that channel as starting material, you can view the actual mask at whatever magnification you like as you make it; this is a solid advantage with some images.

You must search for a color channel that separates the desired features tonally. Duplicate the image and convert the copies to other color modes as needed until you find the best candidate channel. In the "Softer & Softer" image the dots are clearly accessible in the Magenta channel. By duplicating this channel and applying Curves to the new channel as you watch the dot edges, you can quickly create a very accurate mask (Figure 6.8).

In cases where no channel clearly separates the desired region by tone, you will probably have better luck using Color Range. You must decide on an image-by-image basis.

The Perils of Using Masks with Contone Edges

Masks that have contone edges limit your editing options. Even a very accurate mask with soft edges is only partially effective in its soft regions. You should consider this limitation as you plan your edits. Many edits of photographic images involve small changes, where this limitation won't matter much (middle row of Figure 6.9), but if you push the edits too far the limits become more obvious (bottom row of Figure 6.9).

Figure 6.8a
In the Magenta channel, the dots and their edges stand out clearly from the background.

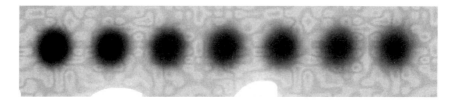

Figure 6.8b
By duplicating the Magenta channel, inverting, and applying Levels, you can quickly build an accurate mask that follows the complex contours of the dots.

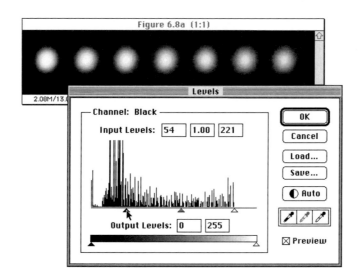

Figure 6.9
(a) The original dots; (b) A moderate change using the mask shown in Figure 6.8b; and (c) An extreme change using the same mask

Making a Frisket Mask to Silhouette a Photo

The photo in Figure 6.10 was shot against a plain background with wash lighting. The following example will silhouette the child and replace the background with something a bit more exciting. You'll need to construct a good basic frisket mask for the child's outline. If you want to do a really fancy job, consider the fine edge detail too.

Figure 6.10
The Magic Wand can't quickly select the background in this image.

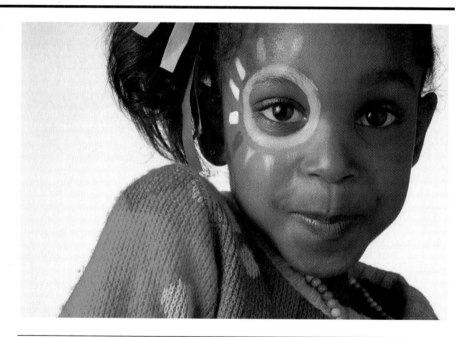

At first glance you'd think that replacing the simple background poses no serious challenge, but on closer examination, problem areas emerge. The wash lighting causes the background to change color, the hair contains subtle detail contaminated by the background color, and to be realistic, the texture of the sweater fuzz should be captured. The areas where the skin meets the background will be easy, but no single color readily defines the other edge areas. In this case no fast set of Magic Wand selections will give us the selection we need (Figure 6.11).

Figure 6.11
Quick Mask reveals that the Magic Wand does fine where the skin meets the background, but this automated tool can't quickly accommodate all the different edges in this image.

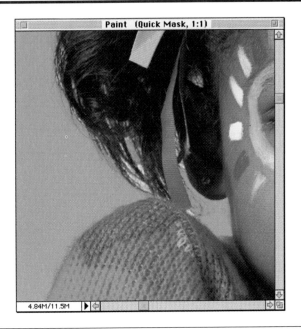

In the following example we'll cover everything except how to place the fine detail in the hair and sweater fuzz. Refer to Chapter 7 for this technique.

The Plan

To replace the background, search for the channel that most evenly separates the girl's outline from the background. Then use that channel as the basis for a silhouette frisket mask.

The background replacement will be done in RGB mode, taking care to keep the new background colors within the CMYK printing gamut. If the background colors were CMYK-critical, such as Pantone or Trumatch swatch colors, the replacement would be done in CMYK so the colors could not shift during the RGB-to-CMYK conversion. Working in CMYK uses a bit more RAM, however, and this may be a consideration for you when you are working with large files.

Finding, Duplicating, and Modifying the Channel

Among the four readily available color modes—grayscale, RGB, CMYK, and Lab—there are 11 channels to choose from. Duplicating the image and making scratch conversions to the other modes allows you to view all the possibilities (Figure 6.12).

Figure 6.12
The various color modes give a total of 12 channels as candidates for masks. For this image, the Blue channel most consistently separates the edges of the subject from the background.

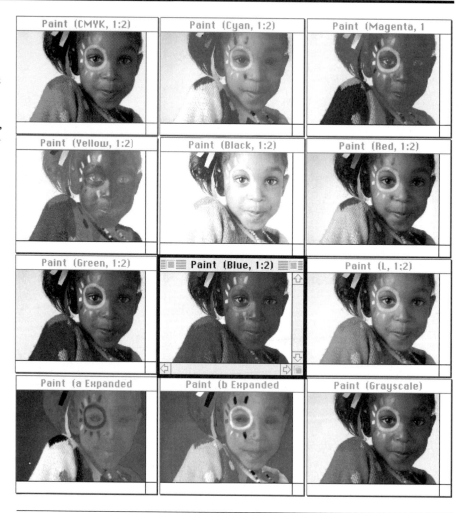

Here's how to make a frisket mask that captures the necessary edge detail as shown in Figure 6.13. After a little practice, you should be able to adjust the edges of these types of masks quickly and easily. You will find that every image offers a different challenge.

In this case, the Blue channel shows nice, even tonal separation of the background from the rest of the image.

- Duplicate the Blue channel into a new alpha channel

- Set the channel's display to a color that contrasts with the image

- Use Curves to modify the new channel's tone

Figure 6.13
You can make this frisket mask quickly by duplicating the Blue channel into a new alpha channel, then viewing this channel while modifying its tone in Curves. The sharper the slope of the curve, the harder the edge of the frisket. Adjust the tone so the background is completely clipped to white and the frisket edge falls within the subject.

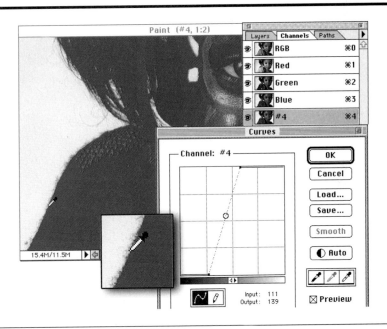

Once the tone is adjusted for the edge you want, you usually need to clean up the inside of the mask and touch up a few edge areas. You can quickly trace inside the edges with the Lasso (Figure 6.14a) and fill with black. To touch up any remaining edge areas quickly, use the Lasso to trace the problem. Then hold down the Command key (to subtract from the selection) and click in the background-color portion of the selection with the Magic Wand (Figures 6.14b and 6.14c). Fill the resulting selection with black. (This is a situation where it makes sense to use the Lasso!) The whole process of making the frisket mask should take you only five minutes or so from the channel selection to the finished mask (Figure 6.15).

Figure 6.14a

After applying Levels to get the frisket mask edges right, you can clean up the interior by selecting it with the Lasso and filling with black.

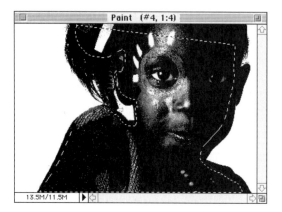

Figure 6.14b

To select edge areas that aren't cleanly defined, you can select their region with the Lasso, then Command-click with the Magic Wand tool.

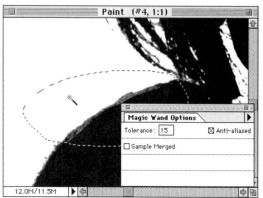

Figure 6.14c

When you Command-click with the Magic Wand in the light area, the selection collapses to conform to the edge, and you can then fill it with black. Adjust the Magic Wand Tolerance as needed, and use anti-aliasing so the filled edge matches the rest of the mask

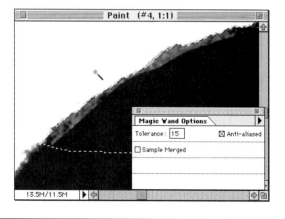

Figure 6.15
Once you practice a few times, the process of making a good frisket mask from an image channel should take you only five minutes or so.

Only in the most extreme cases do you need to make an entire frisket mask using the Lasso tool. You can almost always find at least some regions of an image where you can save time using the above technique.

Checking the Mask

It's always a good idea to check a completed mask before using it. Set the mask channel to display at 100 percent white and view the mask as both positive and negative along with the image. In the "inverse view" (Figure 6.16a), you should see fragments of edge detail outside the mask—these areas are contaminated with the background color, so you need to eliminate them in the frisket mask unless the old and new backgrounds are very close to one another in color. The "positive view" (Figure 6.16b) is a great way to preview an edit without making any changes to the pixels.

Figure 6.16a
By viewing the image and the mask channel together you can evaluate the mask. Here the mask channel is displayed as white with 100 percent opacity. The visible portions of the image will be eliminated from the silhouette.

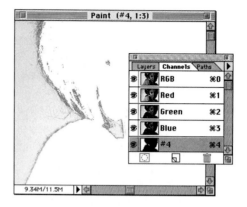

Figure 6.16b
By inverting the mask channel as you display it with the image, you can also review the areas of the image that will be included in the silhouette.

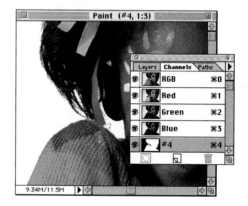

Making the Edit

Once the mask is right, the actual edit is no big deal. Load the frisket mask and edit away! In this case I replaced the background area with a blurred KPT 2.0 Gradient. To avoid visible threadlike artifacts around the frisket edges (where the pixels are only partially selected), I worked separately with the KPT material and pasted it into the selection region for the final image (Figure 6.17). For many situations this image would be acceptable as it stands.

Figure 6.17
The mask is loaded and a new background is pasted into the selection. Although the fine edge detail is lost, this silhouette would be acceptable in many commercial situations.

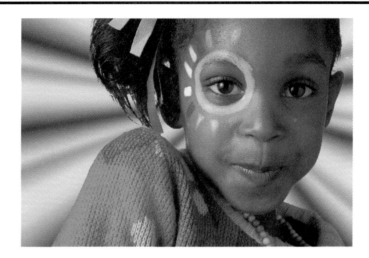

Re-creating the Edge Detail

In cases where extra effort is warranted, you can spend another 15 minutes or so to re-create most of the fine detail that the frisket mask clipped away (Figure 6.18). The techniques for accomplishing this are covered in Chapter 7.

Figure 6.18
Using the techniques described in Chapter 7, you can restore the fine edge detail for a high-quality silhouette.

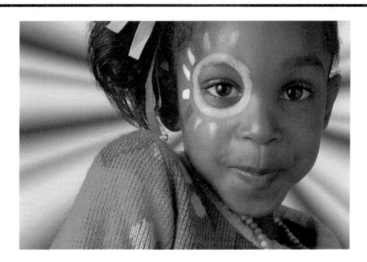

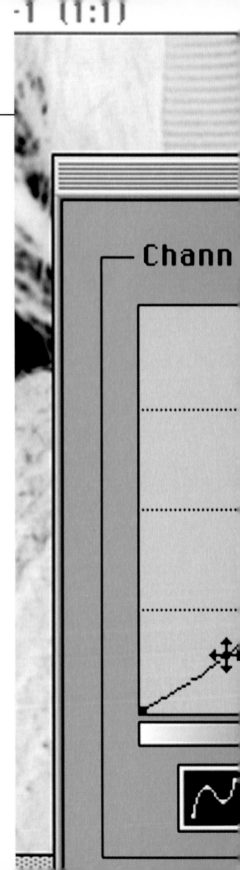

CHAPTER

Soft Silhouettes and Fine Silhouette Detail

Restoring Original Detail

Making the Detail Mask

Soft-Edged Silhouettes

Seldom does a client request that you silhouette a portion of an image and "make it look obvious." Except in a very odd circumstance, you want a silhouette to look as natural as possible given the time you can afford to spend creating it.

Chapter 6 discussed how to make a silhouette frisket mask quickly. In many cases a simple frisket is fine—for example when a figure is placed against a complex background, as in Figure 6.17. There are times, however, when a frisket gets you only part way home.

A very common silhouette assignment is one of the toughest—creating a silhouette of a person or other subject with fine edge detail, and placing the silhouetted image against a plain light background, where the frisket edges will be clear for all to see. As the era of the hand-cut silhouette draws to an end, you need no longer suffer with crude-looking outlines in such cases. With Photoshop you can restore the fine detail the frisket chops away, you can create a soft silhouette edge, or you can do both.

Restoring Original Detail

In this chapter we'll use the same image we used in Chapter 6, but this time the silhouette will end up on a plain white background. We already know that for this particular image, the Blue channel gives us what we need to make a frisket mask. If we simply make a frisket mask as in Chapter 6 and use it to silhouette the little girl's image against a white background (Figure 7.1), the result is better than a hand-cut outline, but it still looks a bit artificial.

Figure 6.16a shows how much detail a silhouette frisket mask can chop away. You may well ask, Why not save this detail by making a better mask? There are two good reasons. First, you can rarely spare

Figure 7.1
A silhouette created using a frisket mask. Some edge detail is lost.

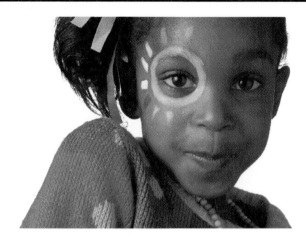

the time to make a frisket mask that could capture all the detail. Second, the detail is tinged with background color, so even if you made a "perfect" mask to capture it, the detail couldn't be used directly in the final silhouette.

In order to put natural-looking edge detail into the final image, you need to take another approach: Make a mask of the edge detail and paint or airbrush into it.

Painting into an Edge-Detail Mask

When you modify a channel to make a frisket mask, as in Figure 6.13, you can modify the tone to suit different needs. For a simple frisket, you adjust the tone so the edge of the mask falls slightly inside the subject, eliminating the background-color contamination that almost always occurs at the subject edge. For a detail mask, however, you modify the tone to emphasize the fine edge detail. In fact, tone modifications are the secret to success.

Once you have captured the edge detail in a mask, you can load the mask as a selection, choose some color from the subject, and airbrush into the selection to restore the edge texture. Or, you can pick up natural texture and color with the rubber stamp and clone this texture into your detail selection. The edge detail in Figure 7.2 was airbrushed.

Figure 7.2
By restoring the edge detail, you can make the silhouette look more natural. Color was picked up from the image and airbrushed using an edge-detail mask.

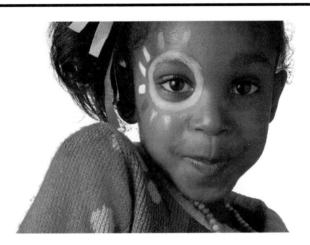

Making the Detail Mask

Here's a procedure for making the edge detail mask used for Figure 7.2. You can modify it as needed to accommodate any image with clearly visible edge detail. First you make an intermediate mask favoring the edge detail, then you multiply this mask by a choked, inverted, slightly blurred version of the silhouette frisket mask. The resulting edge-detail mask allows you to airbrush or clone the detail without affecting the rest of the image.

1. Evaluate the image and decide how to proceed.

2. Make scratch files of the image to search for candidate channels for making masks. Convert these scratch files into other color modes as needed, and examine the individual channels. You will sometimes find that different channels bring out detail in different

areas, depending on the color of the detail and the color of the background.

3. Once you have found the channel(s) that best separates the detail from the background, duplicate the channel as necessary and adjust its tone to emphasize the detail areas (Figure 7.3). To do this, you need to drop the background completely while emphasizing the detail slightly. The more you emphasize the contrast in the detail itself, the less subtlety you leave in the detail mask. (You'll probably want to practice with a few images to get the hang of this.)

Figure 7.3
Find a channel that separates the detail clearly from the background, then duplicate this channel for use in making a detail mask. As the first step in making the mask, adjust the tone to emphasize detail slightly while dropping out the background.

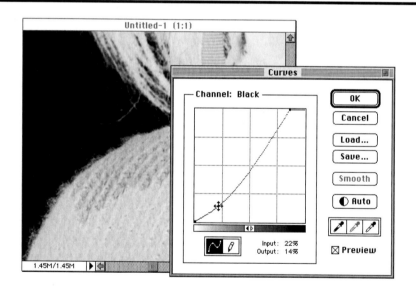

4. Repeat step 3 as needed to isolate detail in various regions at the edge of the silhouette, then combine these intermediate masks into a single mask. You can easily do this by isolating the detail regions so they don't overlap, then performing a Lighter calculation to combine the areas into a single scratch channel (Figure 7.4). I usually name this channel EdgeScratch.

Figure 7.4
Two detail channels with non-overlapping material can be easily combined with a Lighter calculation to make a scratch mask (in this case, EdgeScratch).

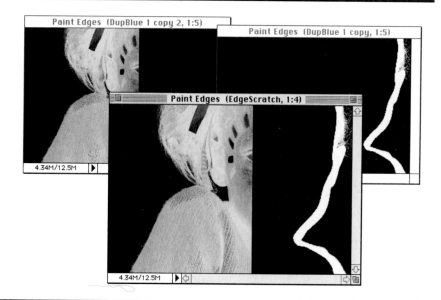

5. Make your silhouette frisket mask using the procedure outlined in Chapter 6. (This may involve the use of a different channel, perhaps from another color mode.) Once the frisket mask is complete, duplicate it.

6. Choke and blur the duplicate of the frisket mask. You can easily choke it by applying Threshold and setting the cutoff level to 1 (Figure 7.5a). Then apply a small-radius Gaussian Blur (Figure 7.5b). The best value of the radius will vary with the image content and resolution. When multiplied with the EdgeScratch mask, this choked, blurred frisket will knock out all but the edge-detail regions. It will also leave a slightly feathered interior edge to help the detail airbrushing blend in with the rest of the image.

7. Multiply the choked-and-blurred frisket mask and the Edge-Scratch channel to make the final edge-detail mask (Figure 7.5c).

Figure 7.5a
Applying Threshold at a low level effectively chokes the frisket mask.

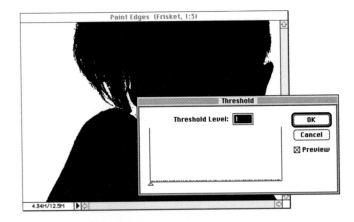

Figure 7.5b
A slight blur at the edge of the choked frisket will create a soft inside edge in the detail mask, which will help blend the airbrushed detail into the rest of the silhouette.

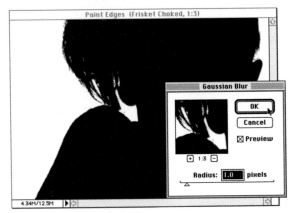

Figure 7.5c
Multiplying the choked frisket and the Edge-Scratch mask from Figure 7.4, you obtain an edge-detail mask with a slightly feathered interior (EdgeMask).

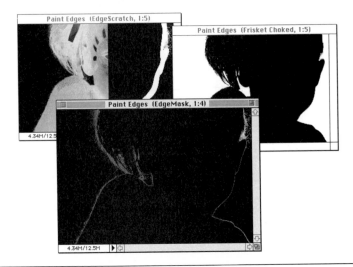

8. After you have created your basic silhouette using the frisket mask, you can load the edge-detail mask and airbrush colors from the subject into the edge regions as needed (Figure 7.6). If the edge-detail regions are large, you might prefer to clone texture from the image using the Rubber Stamp in lieu of airbrushing. Such cloning works especially well with certain styles of hair.

Figure 7.6
By airbrushing color from the subject into the detail mask, you obtain a natural-looking silhouette—and the edge detail blends properly with the background.

Note that since you are painting (or cloning) into a mask, the restored detail evenly blends with whatever background you have used for the silhouette. Practice this technique a few times to get the feel for the tone modifications—they will make all the difference in the world.

Soft-Edged Silhouettes

Sometimes you don't have time to create an entire edge-detail mask, or perhaps the edge detail is so fine that it's a soft blur. In cases like this a soft-edged silhouette can come to the rescue.

The Border command lets you create precise outlines based on selection boundaries. In the Border dialog box, you determine the width of the outline in pixels. You can use this outline as a mask that follows the edge of the silhouette. Applying a blur within this outline gives your silhouette a soft edge. By adjusting the width of the Border and the amount of the blur, you can control the edge softness to suit your needs.

Slightly Feathered Edges

To quickly give a silhouette a slight feathered edge, load the frisket mask you used to make the silhouette. (Apply Inverse if necessary to select the subject, not the surrounding area.) Then apply Border with a small width. The optimum width varies with the content of the image and its resolution. Save the Border selection to an alpha channel to create a border mask.

You'll often find it necessary to edit the border mask to isolate the specific areas where you want the soft edge. It's also a good idea to apply about a 1-pixel Gaussian Blur to the whole mask to soften it, because some minor banding normally occurs in a saved Border outline (see Figure 7.7).

Tip Many images need only a few hints of detail in the right places to look natural. You can often use a slightly feathered edge on most of the silhou-ette, some obvious softness in a few ap-propriate places, and a little edge detail for a good look—and still make your deadline.

Once you are satisfied with the border mask, load it as the selection and apply a Gaussian Blur to the image (see Figure 7.8). This not only provides a soft edge, it also blends the background into the edge for a seamless look. Because the mask already restricts the blur to a border of a specific width, it's best to use a Gaussian Blur radius that is less than the amount of the original Border width—larger radii can produce unattractive effects. For this 300-ppi image, the Border width was 4 pixels, and the Gaussian Blur applied to the image used a 1-pixel radius.

Figure 7.7
To make a frisket mask with a soft-edge silhouette, load the mask, apply the Border command, and Save the selection. The resulting outline follows the edge of the frisket. Touch up the mask to isolate areas that need soft edges, and blur it slightly to smooth out the roughness at the border corners.

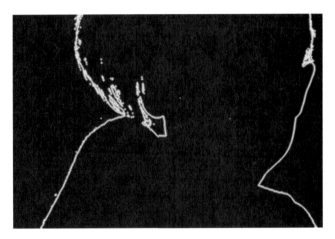

Figure 7.8
To soften the edge of the silhouette, load the cleaned up, blurred border mask and apply a small Gaussian Blur. For this 300-ppi image, the Border width was 4 pixels, and both Gaussian Blur steps used a 1-pixel radius.

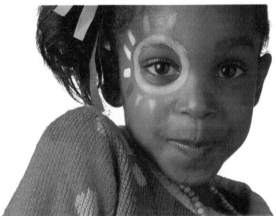

Even Softer Edges

Sometimes you want an obvious soft edge, perhaps for an angora sweater or an animal's fur. In such cases you can simply use a wider Border width and higher Gaussian Blur radius (Figure 7.9). If the Border region is very wide, edit the Border mask to protect areas that should not have a very soft edge, and then perform your blur.

Figure 7.9
A wider Border (12 pixels) and a higher Gaussian Blur (10-pixel radius) combine to give a much softer edge to the sweater.

CHAPTER

8

Drop Shadows and Light Sources

This chapter expands on the basics that were introduced in Chapter 5. It will explain various systems you can use to create drop shadows in your images. We begin by considering the light environment, then discuss basic drop-shadow procedures, drop-shadow parameters, and related approaches to working with drop shadows in Photoshop 3.0.

Most Photoshop professionals use drop shadows to add depth, interest, and a sense of realism to their images. These decisions are often based on what "looks right." No problem, what looks right is the best criterion. If you think systematically, however, you will spend less time experimenting to get that right look.

Airbrush artists have been working with drop shadows for decades. If you are one of these experienced hands, the lighting concepts in this chapter will be familiar. You have probably already discovered that you are ahead of the crowd in the drop-shadow game.

Drop Shadows and Light

We live in an environment of light, and shadows are in action almost everywhere we look. As an artist, you get plenty of practice interpreting shadows and responding to the cues they give; when you view an image, you know intuitively what its shadows say. You must decide whether to go with this—as most will—or to fight it for artistic purposes, which you do at your peril. Either way, you'll be better off if you begin with an awareness of the common expectations. As a rule, common sense plays a major role in drop-shadow work.

Sharp and dull reflections, diffuse highlights, and specular highlights say much about the nature of object surfaces, object shapes, and the light that impinges upon objects. To avoid confusing the viewer, the shadows you construct should be consistent with these other cues to an image's light environment. Does this mean you need to take an hour to mull it all over? Most viewers respond to the totality of a scene and don't notice slight conflicts in lighting cues. When primary cues are in major conflict, however, an image looks wrong (Figure 8.1).

Figure 8.1a
When light and shadow cues are in serious conflict, an image looks wrong. Often viewers can't put their finger on why.

Figure 8.1b
When the shadows make sense, so does the image.

| **Shadows Speak Volumes** | Shadows give the viewer cues about the light environment, including |

- The position of the light source(s)
- The relative intensities of the light source(s)
- The diffusion of the light source(s)
- The position of the object casting the shadow
- The transparency of the object casting the shadow

Drop-Shadow Procedures

The basic drop-shadow procedure presented in Chapter 5, which produces a drop-shadow mask with the shadow-casting object knocked out of it, serves as a reference point for other drop-shadow work. With Photoshop 2.5.1 it is necessary to create such masks, but in Photoshop 3.0 they are needed primarily in cases where you want to apply subtle edits to a shadow area.

Of course, you can always airbrush shadows onto an image when you need just a minimal touch of shadow (use the Behind mode with the airbrush tool to paint only in transparent regions of a layer). For more substantive drop-shadow efforts the following procedures work well. These procedures first capture the outline of the object, then use this outline to create the shadow. In all procedures, the outline starts out as a selection or a frisket mask, which you then either feather (for selections) or blur (for masks). You then offset the selection or mask to create a shadow or a shadow mask. The procedures use different methods to fit the situations for which they are intended.

Some quick drop-shadow tips for Photoshop 2.5.1 advise you to create the drop shadow before you create the object that casts it, a shortcut that is not advisable in careful work. Photoshop 3.0 allows you to have quick drop shadows or fussy drop shadows. With all four of the following procedures you can see the shadow in action before you have to commit yourself to it.

Basic Layers Drop-Shadow Procedure

Photoshop 3.0 makes it easy to create a drop shadow using the following standard procedure, variations of which are published in Adobe's Photoshop manual (the *Beyond the Basics* booklet that ships with the manual), and are likely to appear also in various books and magazines:

1. Copy the layer with the shadow-casting object. Position the new shadow layer just below the original layer.

2. Check the Preserve Transparency checkbox for the shadow layer and fill the layer with black. (Black is applied through the Transparency mask as if it were an active selection.) Delete any unwanted objects.

3. Uncheck the Preserve Transparency checkbox and apply a Gaussian Blur to the shadow layer. If the first blur is unsatisfactory, undo it, specify a different blur radius, and blur again until satisfied with the appearance.

4. Adjust the position of the shadow with the Move tool, varying the layer blending modes and layer opacity as desired until you obtain the shadow effect you want.

5. Plan to merge the shadow layer with the object layer to avoid tying up RAM.

Figure 8.2 illustrates the layers that were used in this procedure along with the results.

This procedure is simple, direct, and effective, and most users will employ it with good results. Its primary advantage, aside from its directness, is that it lets you keep your options open for fine-tuning the drop shadow up until the moment you merge. This procedure is best used when you are working on a fairly small image.

Figure 8.2
The "standard" Layers drop-shadow procedure calls for duplicating an object's layer, preserving transparency and filling the duplicated layer with black, then removing the transparency protection and blurring the layer to give black shadows. This can lead to several shadow layers. Merge layers as needed to free RAM. In complex cases like this one, where shadows overlay other objects, merging may not be an easy solution. See the text for step-by-step details.

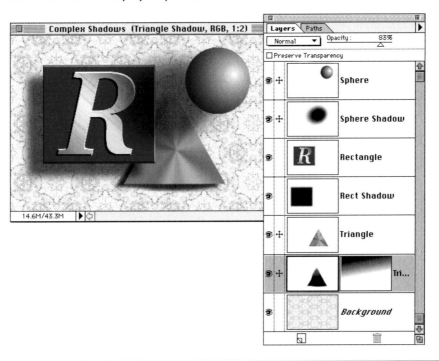

For larger images or constant use this procedure can become inefficient. On a large image the use of a layer's RAM for a drop shadow can be extravagant, and the Gaussian Blur step—applied in three or four channels for color images—can be time-consuming, especially if the extra layer has exhausted available RAM and the blur is applied using the hard disk. The keep-your-options-open advantage dwindles in the face of the RAM-usage penalty. Also, this procedure requires significant use of the mouse, which is bound to try the patience of advanced users who prefer keystroke-based procedures.

The basic procedure may still offer the best choice for complex images with overlapping objects and intricate shadows, but time will often be the trade-off.

Using One Layer for Multiple Shadows

There is a much faster, more RAM-efficient procedure for working with images that contain nonoverlapping objects. This method uses a single layer to hold several drop shadows (Figure 8.3).

1. To hold the image's drop shadows, create a layer immediately above the Background layer and below all other layers. All shadow-casting objects must be in layers above the shadow layer.

2. To get the outline of an object, make its layer active and use Command+Option+T to load the layer's Transparency mask. This instantly and accurately selects all objects in the layer. Deselect any objects you don't want to cast a shadow.

3. Activate the drop-shadow layer (the selection stays active).

4. Feather the selection, then press Command+Option and drag it into position (this moves just the selection).

5. Fill the selection with black and deselect to drop it onto the shadow layer.

Figure 8.3
By placing all drop shadows in a dedicated layer you can work quickly and avoid excessive use of RAM.

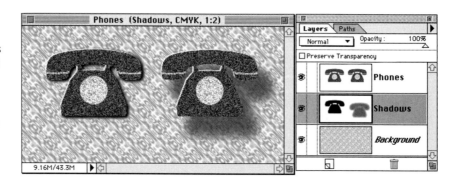

Within the drop-shadow layer you have complete flexibility. To fine-tune the position of an individual shadow, select the region around it and move it. To adjust the opacity of an individual shadow, select the region around it and apply the Eraser tool in Paintbrush mode. To distort or otherwise modify a shadow, select the region around it.

This procedure uses many steps that can be carried out at the keyboard, and it avoids the Gaussian Blur step (feathering is faster, identical in appearance, and uses equivalent radius settings). RAM usage is temporary, and because the shadows remain separate you can readjust them as needed until you flatten the image.

This procedure also requires you to work blind for a moment, feathering and positioning the selection before you fill it, but if you are working with several shadows you will quickly get a sense of how much feathering is needed—and you can easily fine-tune.

Putting the Drop Shadow in the Object's Layer

The most RAM-efficient drop-shadow approach for a multiple-layer image is to paint the drop shadow directly into the shadow-casting object's layer (Figure 8.4). If you paint in a single pass, you get a chance to undo the shadow and try again if you wish. Because this technique uses the layer's Transparency mask, it can't be applied to objects on the Background layer.

1. In the object's layer, use Command+Option+T to select all objects, then deselect any that you don't want to cast shadows.

2. Feather the selection.

3. Make sure a selection tool is active, then press Command+Option and drag (or use the arrow keys) to position the selection for painting.

Figure 8.4
For layers that are not grouped, painting a drop shadow in Behind mode lets you conserve even more RAM and custom-tailor the drop shadow if you wish. You can paint freehand or into a selection, as in this illustration. See the text for details.

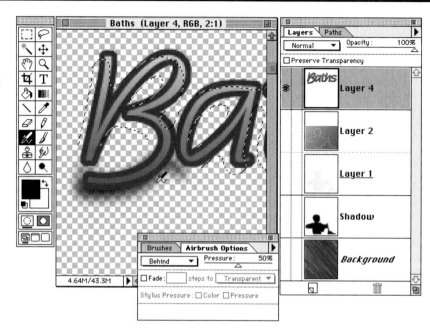

4. Use Command+H to hide the marching ants, make the Airbrush or Paintbrush tool active with Behind mode chosen, and in one pass paint the shadow with black, adjusting the tool's pressure or opacity as needed. (The Airbrush tool lets you paint with more subtlety in a single pass; the Paintbrush tool lets you paint with more consistency.)

5. Immediately use Undo if you don't like the effect, and repeat step 4.

This procedure requires familiarity with the Airbrush tool and a certain confidence, because you get one chance to review the shadow before you commit to it. Because this technique changes a layer's Transparency mask, you can't use it with grouped layers (Figure 8.5).

Figure 8.5
Painting a drop shadow into a layer changes the layer's Transparency mask. If an object is in a grouped layer (as is the human figure), you must put its shadow elsewhere.

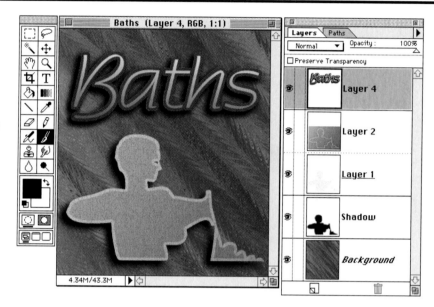

Changing Your Mind One Last Time

If you've committed yourself to a drop shadow in the shadow-casting object's layer but then discover that you just can't live with the effect, don't give up and remake the whole layer. You may have one magic bullet left—the blending sliders. Remember in Chapter 4 (Figure 4.3) how easily the blending sliders omitted all pixels that were colored with black (level 0), making a drop shadow vanish in the process? Assuming your offending shadow is pure black, you can make it disappear by adjusting the This Layer left slider to a value greater than 0. Split the slider (holding down the Option key) to soften any dark gray anti-aliasing artifacts that remain at the shadow edge of the object (Figure 8.6). Assuming you're just going to create a replacement drop shadow (in a different layer, of course) these minor artifacts should be invisible in the final image. Keep in mind that this technique will also eliminate all other completely black pixels. For some images it is therefore inappropriate.

Figure 8.6
If you want to omit a drop shadow in the same layer as the shadow-casting object, you can use the blending sliders in the Layer Options dialog box. Note the positions of the This Layer left slider, split to minimize artifacts in the anti-aliased edges (arrow).

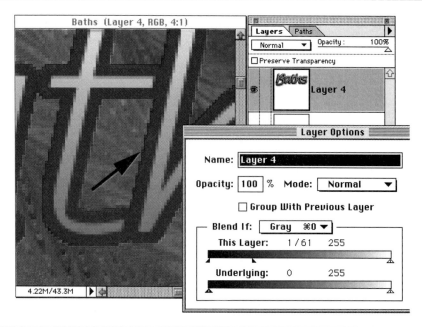

Simple Shadows and Glows in One-Layer Images

No law has been passed requiring the use of more than the Background layer in a Photoshop 3.0 document. Many simple jobs can be done perfectly well—and more quickly—without adding another layer. When working in a single layer you always have the ability use drop-shadow masks like the one in Chapter 5, but Photoshop 3.0 offers you another, faster route.

In Photoshop 3.0 the standard key shortcuts for adding to selections (Shift key) and subtracting from selections (Command key) apply not only to the selection tools but also to the Load command—and to its shortcut that allows you to load a mask by Option-Clicking on its channel in the Channels palette. Thus, by saving a selection in a single channel and making a few clicks and drags, you can quickly build drop-shadow and glow effects.

The following simple technique (illustrated in Figure 8.7) is faster and uses less RAM than layers require. Use layers when you need them and simpler techniques when you don't.

1. Save an accurate frisket mask of the shadow-casting object in a channel.

2. Load the mask by Option-Clicking on the channel name in the Channels palette.

Figure 8.7a
To make a simple drop shadow without using layers, start with a frisket mask (in the "Simple Shadows" channel the light areas are masked). Load the mask as a selection by Option-Clicking on the channel in the Channels palette.

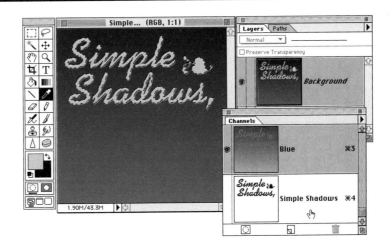

Figure 8.7b
Next, drag the selection, feather it, and float it.

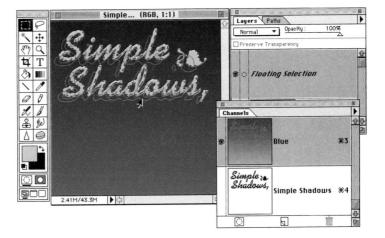

Figure 8.7c
Subtract the material in the mask from the feathered selection by Command+Option-Clicking on the mask's name in the Channels palette. Then fill the remaining parts of the selection—the shadow area—with black. Adjust opacity of the floating shadow selection with single hits on the number keys, then drop the selection.

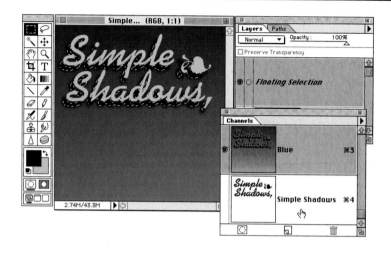

Figure 8.7d
The same technique, without the drag, works for simple glows when you fill with a light color.

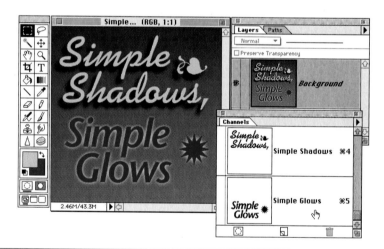

3. With a selection tool active, Command+Option-Drag the selection into position, feather it, and float it.

4. Subtract the mask from the feathered, floating selection by Command+Option-Clicking on the channel name in the Channels palette again.

5. Hide the marching ants with Command+H, fill the selection with black, and (because it's a floating selection) adjust its opacity with the number keys before deselecting.

After you drop the selection you still get a chance to undo the drop and delete the floating selection, of course. For glow effects, use the above procedure without the drag step. The accurate frisket mask is essential, so start with a good selection.

Drop Shadows in CMYK

Chapter 5 notes that in print-production situations you should consider placing drop shadows in the Black channel only. This is especially important to consider when the shadow appears by itself on a white background. If your print production specialist or printer recommends using black-only drop shadows, create them in CMYK. Add them to the Background layer, Black channel only, using the above simple shadow procedure. Photoshop 3.0 won't allow you to write to a single channel within the transparent area of a layer, so you can't use a separate layer for a black-only drop shadow.

Keep the trapping considerations in mind also: Black-only drop shadows can separate from the shadow-casting object if register slips on press. To keep white paper from peeking through, include 20 percent or more black as part of the shadow-casting object if you can.

Drop-Shadow Parameters

Counting the changes applied to the frisket mask of the shadow-casting object, there are six key drop-shadow parameters:

- Resizing the outline
- Gaussian Blur
- Offset
- Shadow intensity
- Light source(s)
- Reflections and highlights

These six will take you as far as you usually need to go in the construction of a shadow. This section discusses the effects of each of these parameters.

Resizing the Outline

Should a shadow mask be a simple blurred frisket mask of the object? Most shadow masks work fine this way, but before blurring the frisket mask, consider the relative positions of the light source, the shadow-casting object, and the background. If the implied light source is close to the object, the shadow might need to be larger than the object's outline. On the other hand, if the object is in the foreground and the background is far away, the shadow cast on the background might need to be smaller than the object's outline. Or, if the plane of the background is angled away from the plane of the object and light source, the shadow might need to be skewed in various ways (note the skewed shadow of the sphere in Figure 8.1b). In all of these cases it's usually easier to make the necessary adjustments to the frisket mask before proceeding with the blur step.

Gaussian Blur

You can quickly create a lifelike shadow mask by applying a Gaussian Blur to a frisket mask of an object. The more you intend to blur, the less precise the frisket outline needs to be.

Consider the shadow carefully before blurring. Higher amounts of blur produce a more diffuse shadow. The more diffuse the shadow, the higher an object seems to float above the background. More diffuse shadows also indicate more diffuse light sources.

Offset

The amount and direction of shadow offset tell the viewer where an object lies in relation to the light source and the background. If you have more than a single drop shadow in a scene it makes sense to place the shadows in separate layers and experiment with their positions until the scene feels right.

Shadow Intensity

How much light diffuses around an object to partially illuminate the background under it? A partially illuminated background requires a less intense shadow. This can grow into a complex calculation, but few artists need ponder it mathematically. Again, what works is what looks right. For cases where you want the colors in the shadow area to change subtly, experiment with the different Layer painting modes and shadow colors (all dark, of course).

Light Source(s)

Photoshop's Lighting Effects filter lets you create complex light sources and cast them on your image. In most situations you still need to attend to the drop shadows, however. Take complex lighting into account as you build the shadows for such scenes (Figure 8.8).

Figure 8.8
Photoshop's Lighting Effects filter lets you build complex lighting effects. Make sure your drop shadows conform to the resulting environment.

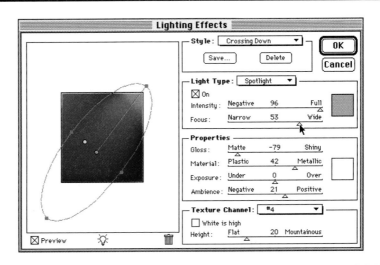

Reflections and Highlights

Finally, reflections and highlights add sparkle to an image. They also give cues about the diffusion, intensity, and placement of light sources. Few viewers are analytical enough to notice slight miscues in reflections and highlights, but you should consider the whole environment as you add these finishing touches.

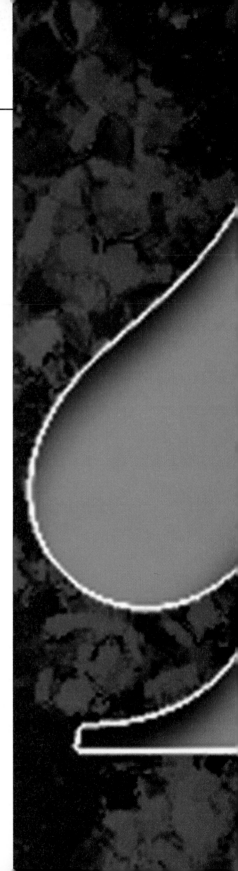

CHAPTER

9

Glows, Recessing, Outlines, and Inlines

low, recessing, outline, and inline special-effect masks may not be as commonly used as the drop-shadow masks discussed elsewhere in this book, but they offer a universe of unique embellishments all their own. Like drop-shadow masks, they start with a mask and a blurred copy of this mask.

As you read this chapter, practice the various mask combinations we discuss. A little bit of experimentation will help you visualize the way these effects are achieved. Whether you create these effects with masks or build them up in Layers, the mask-construction knowledge you gain here will help you every time you need to generate these effects.

This chapter first discusses how to make masks for glows, recessing, outlines, and inlines. It then briefly discusses creating these effects in Layers.

Combinations of Frisket Masks and Blurred Frisket Masks

Let's suppose you have four pieces of film: a positive and negative version of a frisket mask and a positive and negative version of an out-of-focus copy of this same mask. There are four useful ways you can overlay these pieces of film in register on a light table. You can emulate these four combinations in Photoshop by multiplying the masks, as illustrated in Figure 9.1. This produces the typical outglow and inglow masks shown in the Multiply column.

Overlaying the same masks out of register produces the additional effects that are shown in the Offset B column of Figure 9.1. This technique generates both drop-shadow and recessed-shadow masks.

Figure 9.1

You can generate masks for the common glow and shadow effects by multiplying positive and negative versions of a frisket mask and its blurred copy. The typical outglow mask is at the top of the Multiply column, and the typical inglow mask is at the bottom of the same column. If you offset the position of the blurred copy before multiplying, you obtain the shadow masks shown in the Offset B column. Note the positive and negative recessed-shadow masks at the bottom of the Offset B column, and the basic drop-shadow mask at the top of the column.

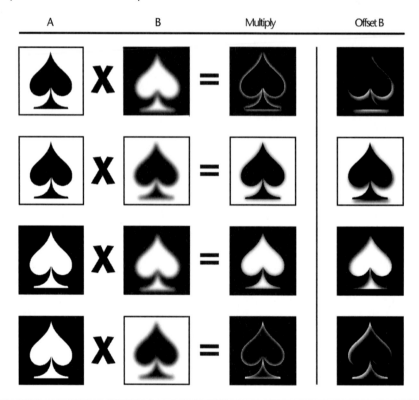

Variations

You can obtain infinite variations on these effects by changing the following: the amount of blur, the amount of offset, the direction of offset, the polarity of the masks, and the amount and type of change you apply as you edit with the masks. Practice making the different masks for a while, then practice using them to apply different effects.

Soft Outline and Inline Masks

The Gaussian Blur filter produces a soft glow that tends to drop out at sharp exterior corners of objects and build up at interior corners. If you seek a more uniform soft outline or soft inline, experiment with the Border command.

By loading the frisket mask as a selection, applying the Border command, saving the resulting selection to a new channel, and then applying the various mask combinations illustrated in Figure 9.1, you can get a range of soft outline and inline effects (Figure 9.2). Vary the Border width according to the line width you desire.

Figure 9.2
Outline and inline masks can be made with the Border command using the copy-modify-multiply approach of Figure 9.1. In the two examples shown here, the original frisket mask (top left) and a negative of that mask (bottom left) are each multiplied with a border mask. These super-impositions result in a soft-outline mask (top right) and a soft-inline mask (bottom right).

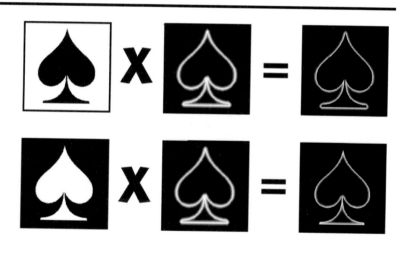

Because Border produces some tone artifacts, it's a good idea to apply a small-radius Gaussian Blur to a Border-generated mask before using it. At high Border width settings, be alert for variations in the width of the outline or inline.

Of course there's no law against varying the offset of a border mask before multiplying it, but most designers prefer the uniform line that you get when you multiply these masks in register.

The Levels Command

Levels excels at modifying masks. Once a mask has been blurred, you can use the Levels command to spread it, choke it, or brighten it up (Figure 9.3). The histogram in the Levels dialog box shows you how tones are distributed throughout the mask, and the Levels controls are just right for most mask-modifying situations. Blur some masks and experiment with modifying them using Levels.

Figure 9.3
The Levels command is very useful for adjusting masks. In blurred areas of a mask, you can use Levels to efficiently spread and choke your image. Here the width of a soft outline mask is adjusted.

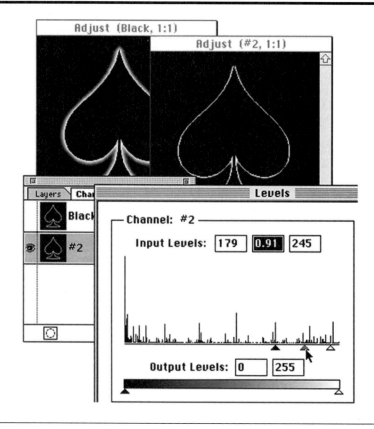

Hard Outline and Inline Masks

Sometimes you will want to create a hard outline or inline (Figures 9.4 and 9.5). In these cases, you can use the Expand and Contract commands or the Maximum and Minimum filters.

Figure 9.4
When you add the Expand and Contract commands or the Maximum and Minimum filters to the copy-modify-multiply approach taken in figures 9.1 and 9.2, you can produce hard outlines and inlines.

To make a hard-outline mask, load your frisket mask, select the area you want to outline, and apply the Expand command to the selection, indicating the desired line width in the dialog box. This creates a spread version of the original selection. You can then save this modified selection into a new channel and multiply this channel with the original frisket mask. The result is a hard-outline mask. To create a hard-inline mask, apply the same technique, but use Contract instead of Expand, and invert the original mask before multiplying. If you prefer working directly with channels instead of with selections, applying the Maximum or Minimum filters will produce similiar results.

Figure 9.5
Selecting the region you want to outline, expanding this selection, and then saving it to a new channel yields the inverted, spread mask seen top row right. The central region in this mask is uniformly larger than the region you selected in the original mask. Multiplying the original mask by this inverted, spread mask is a quick and easy way to generate a hard-outline mask. This mask will have a consistent line width that's derived from the difference between the size of the original region and the size of the spread region.

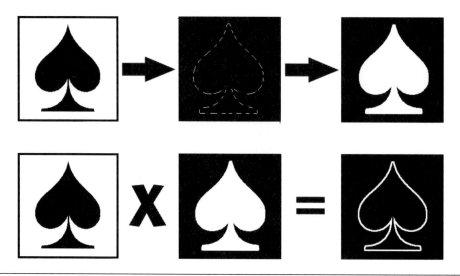

Solid Lines and Production Problems

Whenever you build a solid contrasting line that you ultimately plan on printing, you must consider trapping. The challenge is to compensate for the misregistration that inevitably occurs when multiplate images are printed on a press. Your goal in trapping is to avoid having bare, white paper unintentionally show through your image. Plan to print at least two colors of ink in all places where sharp color transitions occur. In general, try to select colors that have at least 20 percent of one of the process colors in common, or use black and arrange to have it overprint other colors (Figure 9.6). Trapping is an important and involved topic that is outside the scope of this book.

Your Photoshop manual and books that focus on trapping such as *Complete Guide to Trapping* (The Color Resource, 1993), can provide you with more information.

Figure 9.6
The top row of windows shows an untrapped detail area from Figure 9.4. The bottom row shows the same image after it has been manually trapped. Both magenta and yellow inks have been expanded into the area of the black line—the magenta halfway across the line and the yellow all the way.

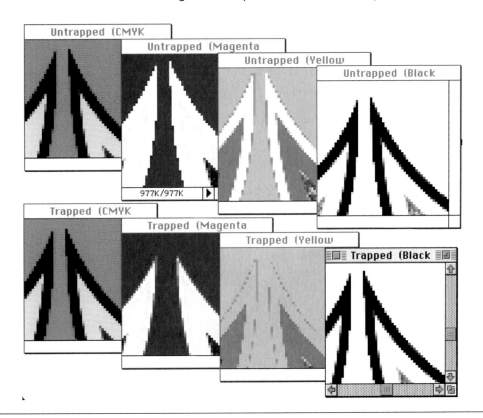

When you imageset your image, the hard lines that are created in Photoshop will be produced at your image's resolution. If you need really clean outlines and inlines, consider importing your images into a vector graphics program such as Adobe Illustrator and generating the outlines and inlines there. Vector graphics, which are based on equations rather than specific pixel-by-pixel descriptions, produce graphics that use the maximum resolution of the output device on which they are printed. The lines they generate are as clean and sharp as your imagesetter can produce. The imported Photshop image will look the same, but the outlines and inlines you lay over it will be sharper and finer than the lines Photoshop can generate.

Creating Effects in Layers

Creating glow and outline effects is a blast with Layers, because you can stack up the effects and try different color edits, positions, and degrees of Layer opacity until you're happy with the result (Figure 9.7). The more you've practiced with the mask combinations at the top of this chapter, the faster your Layers-based sessions will proceed.

Figure 9.7
The fundamental techniques you learn creating mask effects can be directly applied to creating Layer effects. Where Layers can do the job, they are often more flexible than masks because they let you keep your options open.

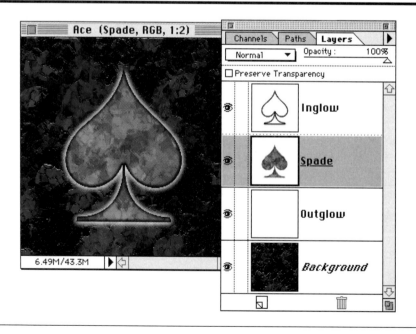

While objects for outlines and outglows stack naturally one on top of the other, using Layers to manipulate inglows can be confusing. The key is to group the inglow object with the layer immediately below it, as in Figure 9.8.

Figure 9.8
The recessed shadow in this layer is actually a dark inglow. Grouping this inglow with the spade layer lets the spade determine the edge of the shadow.

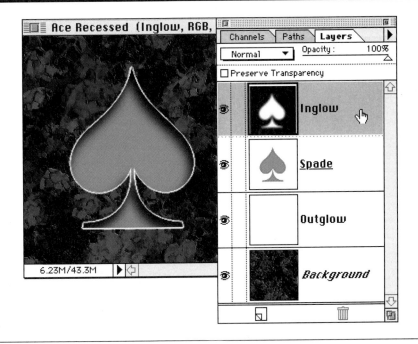

There is one disadvantage to working this way in Layers: You can get carried away with the possibilities and run over your deadlines. Have fun!

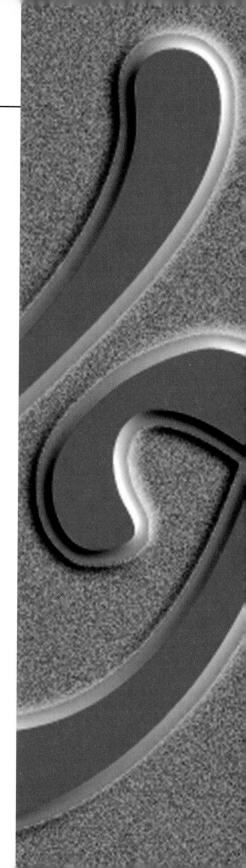

10

Embossing, Relief, and Bevels

The special effect called embossing offers a refreshing break from standard flat graphics. This combined highlight-and-shadow effect requires two masks—one for the highlights and the other for the shadows. With these masks in hand, it's an easy task to use Photoshop to emulate the way light naturally responds when an object is raised out of or pressed into a surface.

Effective embossing can yield striking results. Nonetheless, it calls for a delicate touch, because the interplay of light and shadow on a real embossed image is quite subtle. To produce a convincing embossed effect with Photoshop, you need to pay careful attention to the location and quality of the implied light. You'll often obtain better results if you concentrate on making the embossed effect look believable rather than simply dramatic.

Photoshop allows you to place a sharp boundary at the edge of an embossed object. Your highlights and shadows can appear on the area immediately surrounding the object or on the edges of the object itself. In images where the boundary of an object is clearly defined, this book calls effects that are applied outside the object *emboss effects*, and it calls effects that are applied on the object itself *relief effects*. Emboss and relief effects are very similar but require slightly different techniques and garner different results (Figure 10.1).

Fundamental Technique

When you view an object sitting on a background in a natural setting, you need a light source at a relatively low angle to perceive the height of this object. This light source creates a highlight on one side of the object where the light hits and a shadow on the other side of this object where the light is blocked. Because the object is *sitting on* the background, the object and its shadow are tightly connected. It

Figure 10.1
Effects that are applied outside the object are called emboss effects (left). Effects that are applied on the object itself are called relief effects (right).

is the relationship between the highlight and the shadow that allows us to judge the object's height above its background.

NOTE: *The low angle of lighting that is used in embossing also tends to bring out texture in the surfaces of the object and the background. You can exploit this natural fact to good effect by playing with the way different textures contrast.*

With these principles in mind, it makes sense to generate an emboss effect by using two separate masks—one mask to create the highlights and the other to create the shadows. You can construct these two masks by making a frisket mask that masks out the object you wish to emboss, copying this mask, offsetting, inverting, and optionally blurring the copy, and then multiplying it with the original frisket mask to knock out the area you don't want to edit. When the object to be embossed has a well-defined edge, the resulting emboss masks may resemble very tight drop-shadow masks (Figure 10.2). In general, the two highlight and shadow masks should have the same amount of blurring and offset, but they should be offset in opposite directions. Determine which mask is used to create highlights and which is used to create shadows based on the implied location of your light source. Complete the emboss by loading the highlight mask as a selection and lightening the original image, then loading the shadow mask as a selection and darkening the original image.

Figure 10.2
An emboss effect requires two complementary masks, one for highlights and one for shadows. The amount of blur applied in the process will determine the softness of the embossed edges. Blurring your masks will also help smooth out corners.

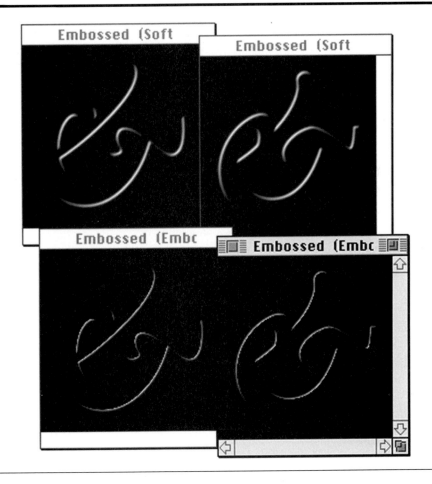

Tip: This technique can easily be modified to create a relief effect. Follow the same steps you used to create an emboss effect, but start with a mask that masks out the region surrounding the object instead of one that masks out the object itself. It may help to keep in mind that the highlight and shadow masks used to produce a relief effect are actually special-purpose inglow masks (Figure 10.3).

As usual, varying the amount of blur and offset will vary your results, but in this case, the range of available variations is relatively narrow. You can't offset the highlight or shadow masks to the point where the highlights and shadows appear to disconnect from the original image or the emboss effect vanishes and the object appears to float.

Figure 10.3
Masks for a relief
effect are actually
special-purpose
inglow masks.

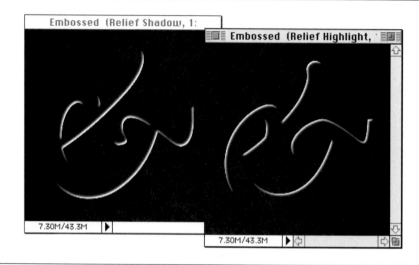

Procedures

Three major avenues can quickly lead you to interesting emboss and relief effects. You can roll your own masks, you can use Photoshop's Emboss filter (though not in the way you might think), and you can use Photoshop 3.0's Lighting Effects filter.

The Standard Procedure

The most flexible (and time-consuming) method for creating emboss and relief effects is to build the necessary masks from scratch by following the technique outlined above. Rolling your own masks this way a few times will enhance your understanding of the general principles involved in producing these effects. It may be helpful at times to brush up on drop-shadow and inglow masks by revisiting Chapters 5, 8, and 9.

Photoshop's Emboss Filter

Photoshop's Emboss filter (Figure 10.4) can give unusual results if you use it directly on an image (Figure 10.5). This filter is designed to flatten the color of an object and generate highlights and shadows. Unfortunately, this approach strips away the original color of your image. Its direct application in the pursuit of emboss and relief effects is therefore limited. Where the Emboss filter really comes into its own is when it is applied to a frisket mask.

The Emboss filter saves you some steps over the standard roll-your-own-mask approach. Using your settings for light angle and pixel height, it handles the amount and direction of offset and generates a mask that you can readily duplicate and convert into both highlight and shadow masks (Figure 10.6). If you discover that the mask the Emboss filter creates lacks tonal range, you can easily increase the Amount setting to enhance the filter's effect.

Figure 10.4
Photoshop's
Emboss filter
uses your chosen
light angle and
pixel height to
automatically cal-
culate highlights
and shadows. The
Amount slider
allows you to
deepen the effect.

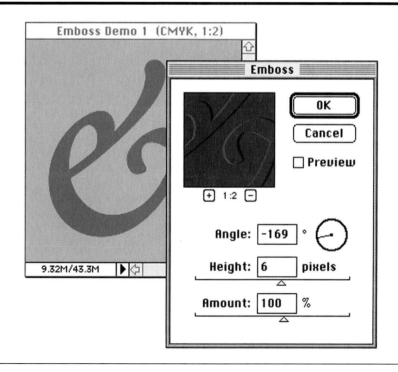

Figure 10.5
Applying the Emboss filter directly to an image (left) can produce a more jarring and unnatural result (center) than you might achieve if you generated a similar effect by constructing your own masks (right). However, the Emboss filter can be quite useful when applied to embossing or relief masks rather than to the original image.

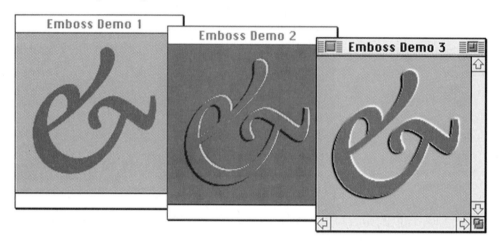

Figure 10.6
The Emboss filter applied to a blurred frisket mask produces an image like this, which you can duplicate and modify to create both highlight and shadow masks.

You'll need to modify the mask that the Emboss filter produces, but it is well worth the 30 seconds that this takes. Start by duplicating the channel that holds the Emboss filter mask. You now have two identical alpha channels. One channel will serve as the highlight mask, the other will become your shadow mask. You need to invert one of these channels and modify the tone of both channels with the Levels or Curves commands. This technique may sound a little complex, but in fact, the whole effect can be quickly applied by taking the following six basic steps:

1. Prepare a frisket mask that masks out the object(s) you wish to emboss or masks in the object(s) you wish to show in relief.

2. Duplicate this mask and, if desired, apply a Gaussian Blur to the duplicate. Different amounts of blur have dramatically different effects. You may want to experiment a few times to determine how much blur is right for your image. Usually a pixel radius of 1 to 6 is a good place to begin, but this will vary depending on your image's resolution. Blurring your mask will ultimately smooth out the edges and corners of your edited image.

3. Apply the Emboss filter to the duplicate of the frisket mask. This produces an image similar to the one shown in Figure 10.6.

4. Duplicate this new mask and apply the Invert command to the copy. Because the Emboss filter produces a mask that is centered on a midtone gray, this inversion simply toggles all shadows to highlights and all highlights to shadows.

5. Now apply the Levels or Curves commands to both copies, forcing all tones below middle gray to be full black. You can do this very quickly in Levels by simply opening the dialog box, typing **128**, and clicking on OK. In Curves, the same result can be achieved by making a simple clipping adjustment (Figure 10.7). Both approaches yield rough highlight and shadow masks (Figure 10.8).

Figure 10.7a
Modify the tone in your highlight and shadow masks by using the Levels command.

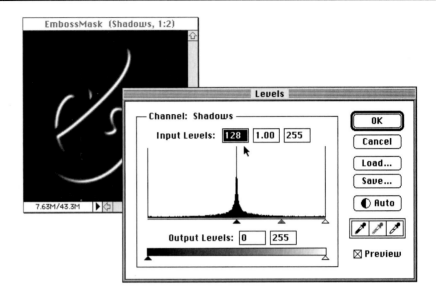

Figure 10.7b
You can also use Curves to get the same result by making the tone adjustment shown here.

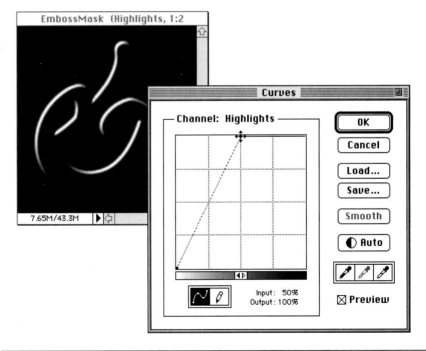

Figure 10.8
A few simple tone adjustments to the original embossed mask can produce both highlight and shadow masks.

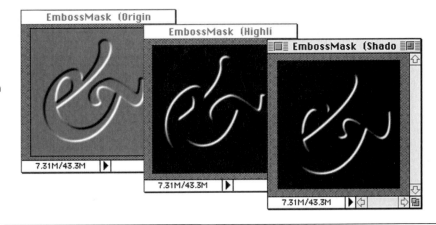

6. To trim these rough highlight and shadow masks, multiply each mask by the original frisket mask. This cleans up emboss masks by knocking out the shape of the original object (Figure 10.9). The same approach, with the original frisket mask inverted, will clean up relief masks by knocking out of the shape of the surrounding region. In both cases, this last step serves to restrict your effects to the well-defined regions you wish to edit.

Figure 10.9
You can multiply the rough highlight and shadow masks by the original frisket mask to produce masks with a well-defined edge.

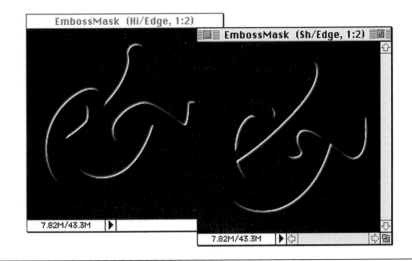

Tip: Regardless of how you produce your emboss or relief masks, you have a range of attractive options once the masks are complete. Experiment with different treatments of texture inside and outside the original frisket-mask outline. You can also try applying two (or more) emboss or relief effects to the same image by stacking them up one within another. This approach can create some very interesting and striking images (Figure 10.10).

With the masks, add highlights and shadows to your image by filling with white and black, respectively, or by making tone adjustments with the Levels command. Airbrush details as needed. You can also "stack" emboss effects, using two sets of masks (Figure 10.10).

Figure 10.10
The stacked-emboss effect, in which one emboss effect is placed on top of another, offers many striking options.

The Lighting Effects Filter

A third approach uses Photoshop 3.0's Lighting Effects filter. Instead of modifying the frisket mask of an object to make highlight and shadow masks, this method involves using the frisket mask as the Texture Map within the Lighting Effects dialog box (Figure 10.11). By adjusting the settings this dialog box offers, you can create impressive embossing and relief effects (Figures 10.12 and 10.13).

The Lighting Effects filter easily creates the effect of light shining on your image. To achieve flatter lighting you'll need to practice with this filter or use one of the other two approaches for creating emboss or relief effects discussed above.

Figure 10.11
The Lighting Effects filter provides many options for adjusting lighting. By using a frisket mask as a Texture Map, you can easily emulate light shining over a specific contour to create impressive emboss and relief effects.

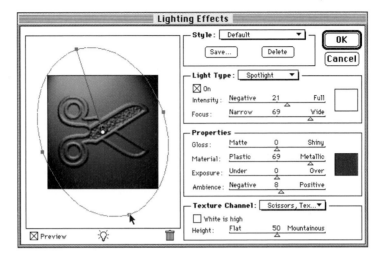

Figure 10.12
The Texture Map approach allows you to use any grayscale image to define highlights and shadows. Here, noise was used within the scissors blade.

Figure 10.13
Intricate frisket masks also work well as texture maps.

Bevels

Why have a plain old flat edge on an object when you can add depth and realism with a bevel edge? You can create a wide variety of bevels by combining basic selection techniques, the Emboss filter method described earlier in the chapter, and some standard calculations. Where the bevel masks are frisket masks, we call them hard bevel masks. Where the bevel masks are contone masks, we call them soft bevel masks. Although the name *soft bevel mask* may seem to be a bit of a contradiction in terms, it will help you keep in mind the related techniques that go into constructing these effects.

Because bevels are related to embossing, you need one set of masks for the highlights and one set for the shadows. As you tweak selections, each set may end up including several masks before you're satisfied with the resulting bevel. In cases where the job warrants this amount of effort (it takes 10 to 20 minutes in a typical situation), the visual effect often wins applause.

By their definition, bevels occur at the edges of objects, so you often need to construct a mask that defines the edge as well as the highlights and shadows. It is the combination of the edge mask and the highlight and shadow masks that produces the bevel.

Making Bevels

Both exterior and interior bevels can vary in edge roundness and softness (Figures 10.14, 10.15, and 10.16).

Figure 10.14
The metal plate in this logo has a standard hard-edged, squared-off exterior bevel. Note the diagonals at the corners of the bevel edge.

Figure 10.15
This version of the logo has a rounded exterior bevel on the outside of the plate and hard-edged interior bevels on the letterforms. Note the diagonals at the interior corners of the letterforms.

Figure 10.16
This version of the logo has soft bevels on the outside edge of the metal plate and on the inside edges of the letterforms. Note the lack of diagonals.

The Most Basic Bevel

The standard hard-edged bevel is often the type that first comes to mind when you think of bevels. Ironically, this bevel requires considerable manual processing to create the hard diagonal edges at the bevel corners. Photoshop's mathematical processes can't read your mind to see the places where the edges should have a hard corner, so you have to put these diagonals in place yourself, usually with the Lasso tool. In a standard exterior four-cornered bevel, this takes just a few moments, but for complex interior bevels, the work can become quite time consuming.

Here's the procedure for building a standard hard-corner, hard-edged bevel:

1. Define the borders of the image you are constructing by selecting the outline within which your object and bevels will fall. Then, by holding down the Command key, subtract the inner, nonbeveled portion of the object from the selection. This leaves just the bevel region selected. Save this as a mask, which we will refer to as the bevel outline mask (Figure 10.17).

Figure 10.17
The bevel outline mask serves as the starting point for making a pair of hard-edged bevel masks.

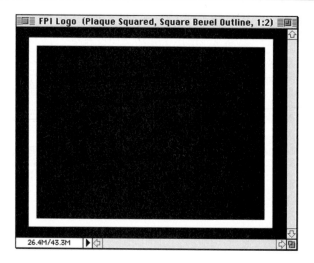

2. Duplicate the bevel outline mask and manually remove two opposing sides, cutting clean diagonals. To perform this edit, use the Lasso tool with anti-aliasing. It helps to hold down the Option key to take advantage of the straight lines in the Lasso tool's rubber-band mode. As you'll see, this is all the diagonal-line editing you need to do.

3. Perform a Difference calculation between the bevel outline mask and the mask containing only the two opposing sides. This will give you a third mask that contains the other two opposing sides (Figure 10.18).

Figure 10.18

Carefully edit the diagonals on a copy of the bevel outline mask to create a mask that defines opposite sides of the bevel (center). By using the Difference calculation, you can easily generate the other opposite-sides mask (right). Then airbrush light and dark color into the bevel edge as needed.

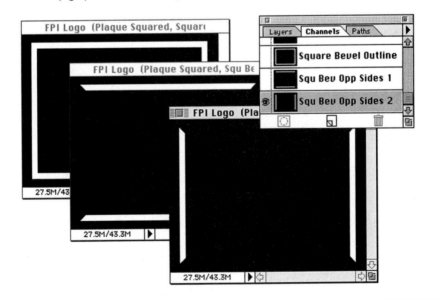

Tip: If you were editing an image with an odd number of sides, you could get the result outlined in this procedureby selecting alternating sides rather than opposing sides. Keep in mind that your goals are to define the hard corners of your bevels and to replicate the natural impact light will have on your beveled surface.

4. Load one of the masks with opposing sides, and edit or airbrush as necessary to achieve the bevel effect you desire. There are various ways to speed up this process. For example, you can edit just one side at a time with Levels (you deselect the other side first, of course). Then repeat the process with the other mask.

5. The opposing-sides scheme lets you edit one side of each corner at a time. As a final touch-up, airbrush contrasting tone into these important hard-corner regions.

Rounded and Soft Bevels

Rounded and soft bevels trade hard corners and well-defined edges for curved corners and soft edges. To create rounded and soft bevels, begin by applying the Emboss filter technique discussed earlier in this chapter to the object you want to bevel. Once you have created emboss masks for highlights and shadows, you can easily edit them to put the bevel edges in place (Figure 10.19).

You can adjust the width of the bevel very efficiently by loading the original frisket mask of the beveled object and applying Expand or Contract to this selection as the situation requires. When both the inner and outer edges of the bevel are knocked out, the result is the two hard-edged rounded masks seen at the bottom of Figure 10.19. You can generate a soft-edged rounded mask by choosing not to knock out the inner edge and instead leaving it diffuse.

Load the highlight and shadow masks in turn, editing each one with Levels and airbrushing highlights into them as needed. It's a considerably faster process than using hard-corner bevels, especially for images that require intricate interior bevels.

Figure 10.19

The two masks at the top were produced by applying the Emboss filter technique to a frisket mask in the shape of a plaque. The resulting highlight and shadow masks were then edited in two steps to produce the two ready-to-use bevel masks at the bottom. First the plaque outline was loaded and the area outside the selection was knocked out. Then the Inverse command was applied to the selection, which was then contracted, and the area inside the contracted selection was knocked out. The bevel width is determined by the number of pixels specified in the Contract dialog box.

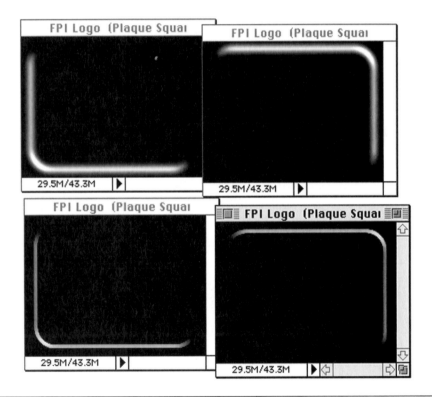

Your bevels get better the more you experiment. For starters, here are some key parameters you should vary as you explore the bevy of opportunities:

- The radius of the initial Gaussian Blur before you apply the Emboss filter.

- The settings in the Emboss filter dialog box. Take 10 minutes just to explore these to see their influence.

- The width of the bevel region.

Notes on Airbrushing

There's something very satisfying about airbrushing into a well-constructed bevel mask. You're free to experiment with adding highlight and shadow touches that make the edge of the image come alive, especially when working with surfaces that have a metal character to them, like the ones illustrated in this chapter. If you examine Figures 10.14, 10.15, and 10.16 carefully, you'll notice many variations in the bevel tones.

A few specific notes:

- In Figure 10.14 the bevel surfaces were entirely airbrushed—the opposing-sides hard-bevel masks didn't allow quick Levels adjustments for tone, because in such masks one side is a highlight and the other side is a shadow. Using full white and full black at 10 percent opacity with a large, soft brush, I built up the edges, making sure there was contrasting tone at all four corners. As always, keep in mind the location and quality of your implied light source.

- Figure 10.15 required just a slight airbrush touch in the upper-right corner of the rounded outside edge bevel; other adjustments to this bevel were performed via Levels using the masks illustrated in Figure 10.19. The inside bevels were another story. These required lengthy manual selection and airbrushing to catch the hard interior corners of the letterforms.

■ Figure 10.16 required airbrushing at the upper-right corner of the soft, round exterior bevel to bring out a natural soft highlight that's consistent with the implied lighting of this illustration. Otherwise Figure 10.16's edits were performed entirely with Levels.

CHAPTER

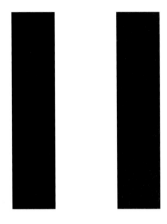

Metal

Creating Metal Surfaces

Timid about trying a metal effect? Don't know how to shift from one metallic look to another? Don't be discouraged. Metal is tough to do—until you know the secrets. The techniques that this chapter covers will show how to quickly produce different metal effects.

Before you read on, consider the following qualities that are associated with metals:

■ Metals are opaque.

■ Some metals don't hold a shine as well as others due to rapid corrosion; this affects the way they are typically finished.

■ We evaluate a metal's appearance by its surface reflections (tone) and its color.

For example, gold, silver, platinum, brass, and chrome don't corrode quickly, so they can be polished to a shine. We tell these metals apart by their color and their luster (luster boils down to holding a shine a little less well). Aluminum, on the other hand, corrodes rapidly if polished, so it is usually brushed to give it a satin-like appearance.

Metals with a shine produce hard, tonally extreme reflections. Metals with a satin finish produce reflections with softer tone. In both cases you can create the tone treatment you need in the Curves dialog box. If you want to produce a natural-looking metal with a specific color, you can assign the color before applying Curves and tweak the color afterwards as well.

Creating Metal Surfaces

Until computers came along, good-looking metal required airbrush work or complex photography. Today, metal can be a part of every Photoshop artist's repertoire. This dazzling effect is sitting right there in the Gaussian Blur filter, the Difference calculation, and the Curves command, waiting for you to set it free.

Before you begin, think about which metal you want to mimic. Does it have a hard shiny look, a soft, satin look, or does it fall somewhere in between? What is its color? Once you have a certain appearance in mind you can proceed with purpose, which will often get you close to the look you want rather fast. And once you're in Curves, you may discover an even better look than you initially imagined.

Basic Procedure for Neutral Metal

The dramatic changes in tone that you'll be making in Curves can create undesirable color changes if you're working in RGB or CMYK color modes. For neutral metals, work in alpha channels until you get the look you want, then copy the metal (still perfectly neutral, since it's grayscale) into the RGB or CMYK image. Here's the typical procedure.

1. Make a frisket mask in the shape you want to render in metal.

2. Save this mask in an alpha channel and duplicate it twice into two new alpha channels. Apply Gaussian Blur to these two copies and offset them in basically opposite directions (Figure 11.1). The amounts of the blurs, amounts of the offsets, and directions of the offsets are variations you should explore.

3. Apply a Difference calculation to the two blurred and offset channels. The result is a difference mask that yields the classic metal effect. Apply Invert to this mask to see the metal effect more clearly. Depending on the amounts of blurring and offset you used, you will get various effects, but the general appearance will resemble Figure 11.2.

Figure 11.1
A metal effect begins in a familiar way. Create two duplicates of a frisket mask, apply Gaussian Blur to both duplicates, and then offset the blurred masks in opposite directions.

Figure 11.2
In this illustration, the difference masks at top and bottom vary only in the amount of Gaussian Blur applied to the intermediate masks.

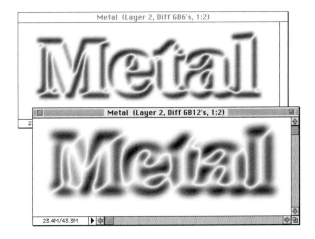

4. To accurately gauge the metal appearance as you modify the tone, you need to see the edges of the original frisket mask. Display the frisket-mask channel over the difference-mask channel, and prepare to apply Curves as shown in Figure 11.3.

Figure 11.3
To accurately show the shape of the metal effect, the frisket-mask channel is displayed over the difference-mask channel. Here the difference-mask channel's display is set to black with 100 percent opacity so that it accurately depicts the channel data. The Master channel display is set to medium gray with 100 percent opacity so that it clearly shows the mask edge. Here the eyedropper samples the midtones.

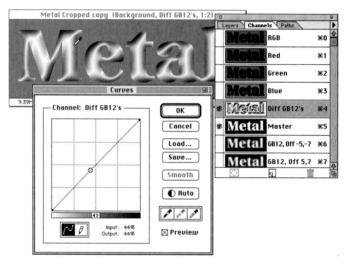

5. Try different curves until you get the metal effect you want. This is one case where moderate curves aren't necessarily the best way to go. By dramatically adjusting the tone in Curves, you can produce a complete range of metallic surface textures from satin to chrome. See Figures 11.4 through 11.7 for examples and comments.

6. Once you get the effect you want, load the frisket-mask channel as a selection in the metal-effect channel. This will define the edges of your metal effect. Copy this effect to the Clipboard and paste it into your image, positioning it as needed. Since it's coming from a grayscale channel it will be completely neutral in color.

Figure 11.4
Experiment in Curves to learn how to control the metal look. For a soft look, moderate tone adjustments can bring out the highlights and midtone shadows that say "satin."

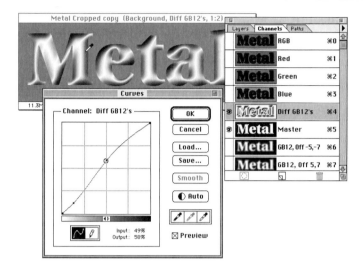

Figure 11.5
Folding the tone curve back on itself gives a harder look. Many different appearances will result from small adjustments to this type of curve. You must experiment, but it usually takes only a minute or two to get an exciting effect.

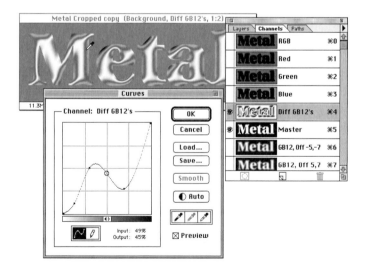

Figure 11.6

A more severe tone curve gives a harder look. To maintain a slightly brushed appearance, the shadow tones in this illustration are adjusted so they don't become fully black.

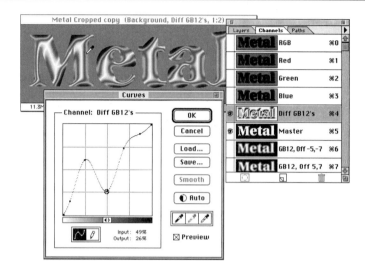

Figure 11.7

A double-hump tone curve delivers more activity in the metal contours, implying a more complex light environment. You can adjust this type of curve in infinite ways to get a harder or softer metal. Experiment, varying the position and height of the humps and the position and depth of the valleys. Also try a three-humped curve for extreme activity.

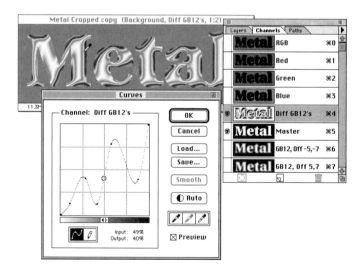

General Guidelines

Once you know the basic technique, a few guidelines are all you need to construct exciting metal effects:

- To get a better idea of how the effect works with other image elements, you might prefer to adjust the metal look within your image, rather than just in the alpha channel. You can do this if you first convert your image to Lab color and then apply the large tone changes to the Lightness channel only (with the metal area selected via the frisket mask, of course).

- Instead of applying the Curves changes to the entire difference mask (as shown in step 4 above) you might be tempted to simply load the frisket mask and only apply the changes to the area you plan to use. This will work fine in some cases, but in others the tonal changes are so large that anti-aliased or feathered edges in the frisket mask may produce odd artifacts at the very edge of the metal surface.

- Gentler tone transitions give softer looks to the metal. When you're going for a soft look, pay special attention to the highlights—this is where the first critical tone transitions occur. On the other hand, when you're going for a shiny look pay special attention to the shadows, as these are darker due to the *specularity*, or mirrorlike quality, of the reflections on a shiny surface.

- The Curves dialog box can only amplify the tones and contours already present in the difference mask. These starter tones will vary a great deal as you change the amounts of Gaussian Blur and Offset in the two masks to which you apply the Difference calculation. Smaller Gaussian Blur radii and smaller Offsets in these two masks tend to produce a metallic contouring that is confined more to the edge of the frisket mask (Figure 11.8). Experiment with the Gaussian Blur and Offset variations. The results they produce are quite impressive.

Figure 11.8

You can control how deeply the metal effect reaches into the metallic area by varying the Gaussian Blur radius in your intermediate masks. Here the Gaussian Blur radius applied to the intermediate masks was 6, as opposed to the radius of 12 applied the intermediate masks used for the previous illustrations. The tonal curve in this illustration is identical to that used in Figure 11.7, but the metal effect is confined more closely to the edge of the letters.

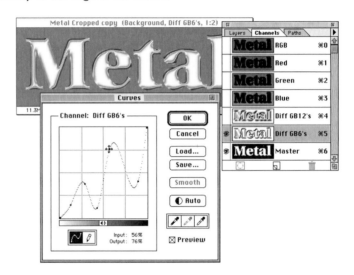

Colored Metal

If you need to give the impression of a colored metal, you need to work in Lab color as you make the large tone modifications. There are various ways to do this. The simplest approach is to convert your image to Lab color and work with the metallic region as you would with any other selected region, applying tone modifications with abandon. In other cases you won't want to casually convert to Lab (especially if you are working in CMYK), so you can use the following procedure in place of steps 4–6 above:

1. Load the frisket mask of your desired metallic region, and edit the resulting selection to produce a color close to that of the metal you are imitating.

2. With the selection still active, copy it to the Clipboard.

3. Create a new file. Select Lab Color from the Mode pop-up menu in the New dialog box. The pixel dimensions for this new image will match those of the object in the Clipboard (in this case, your metallic region).

4. Paste your metallic region into the new Lab image. As you paste, Photoshop converts color mode automatically, so the metallic region will now be in Lab color mode.

5. Perform the Curves modifications as needed to produce your desired metal look.

6. Move the metallic region back to your original image via a cut-and-paste or drag-and-drop operation, depending on the version of Photoshop you are using and the way you like to work. As the Lab metallic region re-enters your original image it will automatically convert back to that image's color mode.

After you have applied the tonal changes to your colored metal, you will probably want to make minor color adjustments. Use the Hue/Saturation command to touch up the hue, saturation, and lightness of the metal as needed. Small changes usually work best if you seek natural-looking metal. If you are producing a metal with an artificial color, anything goes (Figure 11.9).

Speaking of artificial effects, colorizing a neutral metal region can produce striking zebra-color effects (Figure 11.10).

Reflections

Polishing a surface makes it specular, or mirrorlike. The shinier the surface, the harder and more specular the reflections the surface produces. Conversely, the more contoured the surface, the more distorted the reflection. In fact, even slight contours in a highly polished metallic object cause major distortion (the funhouse-mirror effect).

Figure 11.9
Once you have adjusted colored metal in Lab mode, you can modify its color liberally using the Hue/Saturation command.

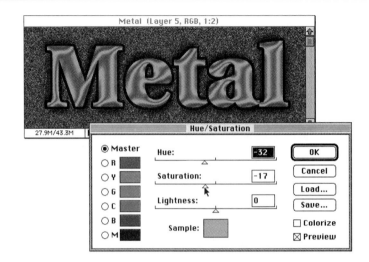

Figure 11.10
Colorizing a grayscale metallic image after the tonal variations are completed can produce striking zebralike results.

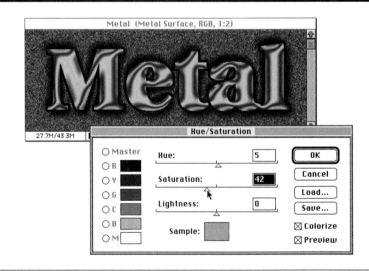

The nature of your image will determine whether you should give the impression that some sort of reflection is present. As a rule you can add reflection interest to the metallic region by adding a few soft blobs of moderately dark tone just before applying your heavy tone changes in Curves. Give the reflection blobs about the same tonal value as the shadow areas in the difference mask. If you wish to mock up a colored reflection, add the reflection blobs in logical colors and perform the tone changes in Lab as described above.

CHAPTER

12

Adding Noise and Sharpening

The Beauty of Noise

Sharpening

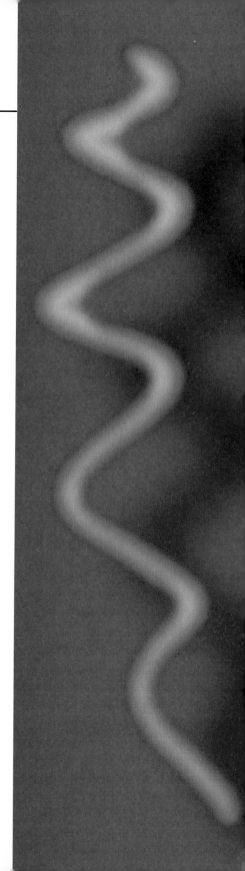

oise is a topic that is so elegant in its simplicity that we often forget about it. In the form of fundamental low-level randomness, noise exists in all aspects of nature and life. In Photoshop images, you'll often encounter noise in the form of the natural variations in color that are caused by any of the following factors: photographic grain, characteristics of the scanner, or perhaps even minute variations in the original subject. Far from being offensive, as long as this noise remains subtle, it can help make your image look more vital and more natural.

One of the few areas where noise can be completely—and artificially—eliminated is in the computer's description of an image. However, when you want to reproduce the image or show it to an audience outside the digital realm, this image must be converted into analog form. As it enters the physical, analog world, the image becomes subject to all the natural rules of that world, including the imposition of noise. The image also encounters an underlying natural presumption that it contains noise. As you will see, if noise is not evident in an image, the quality of the image may suffer.

The Beauty of Noise

Examine a uniform-looking area of a photograph at high magnification in Photoshop. You'll notice that the pixels making up this "uniform" area are not all identical. Except for regions where the image data has been artificially clipped or compressed, there is some random character to the pixels. Examine a small region closely and you might be surprised at the variation (Figures 12.1a and 12.1b).

Figure 12.1a
The boy's arm appears uniform in color in the area enclosed by the square.

Figure 12.1b
A close-up view (left), and the same close-up view with tonal range greatly enhanced via Levels Auto (right), show natural variation—noise, and in this case some subtle JPEG tiles too.

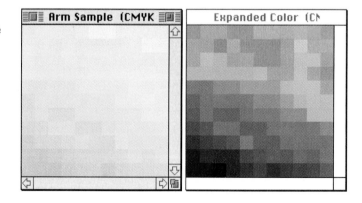

An image with no noise can feel unnaturally flat (Figure 12.2). Add some noise in the right places and it tends to perk up (Figure 12.3). To this end, Photoshop offers noise in two flavors: Uniform noise and Gaussian noise.

Figure 12.2
This relatively flat image contained no noise in its Photoshop form. Of course, a small amount of noise was certainly introduced in the prepress and printing processes.

Figure 12.3
The same image as in Figure 12.2, with noise strategically added in Photoshop, has more life.

Photoshop Noise

Photoshop noise randomly changes the levels of pixels within a limit you set. From the Noise dialog box you can apply Uniform noise or Gaussian noise in amounts ranging from 1 to 999. The Amount values correspond to levels, but they actually determine an allowable range of random level variation.

To see the difference between the two Photoshop noise distributions, apply some noise to a flat gray area, then look at the area with the Histogram function. Photoshop's Uniform noise is applied to all selected pixels within a range of levels determined by the Amount setting. Outside this range, no noise is applied at all (Figure 12.4). When you apply Gaussian noise, the situation is a bit more complex. Photoshop applies Gaussian noise with a soft fall-off in a bell curve. This is a naturally random distribution (Figure 12.5).

Figure 12.4

A Photoshop histogram of an area that started as an even 50 percent gray, to which Uniform noise of Amount 20 was then applied. The histogram shows that the level of each pixel is allowed to vary randomly within a strict limit of 20 levels. Within this limit, all amounts of variation are equally likely, but outside the limit no variation occurs at all.

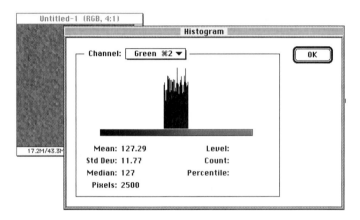

Figure 12.5

A Photoshop histogram of the same 50 percent gray area, but this time Gaussian noise of Amount 20 was applied. With Gaussian noise, the 20-level limit is not strict, but smaller variations are more likely than larger ones. This bell-curve distribution is very common in nature.

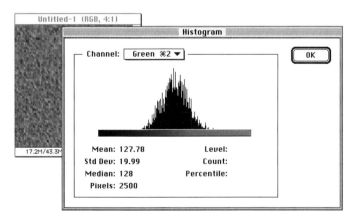

Both types of noise have their uses. Uniform noise has less natural graininess than Gaussian noise. If you want the most natural look, theoretically you should use Gaussian noise—but as always, your eyes should be the judge. The more regular distribution found in Uniform noise makes it ideal for overcoming potential image problems such as banding.

Because applying noise tends to make individual pixels stand out, the look you get with different amounts of noise will vary depending on the resolution of your image (Figure 12.6).

Figure 12.6
At lower resolutions, the visual impact of noise increases. This image is a lower-resolution version of the image used for figures 12.2 and 12.3. It contains the same Photoshop noise distributions and amounts as Figure 12.3.

Other Noise Filters

Photoshop's noise filters also include Despeckle, Dust and Scratches, and Median. Despeckle and Dust and Scratches are designed to provide fixes to specific image problems. All five noise filters can be useful tools for generating random textures. Experiment with combining Uniform noise and filters such as Crystallize, Find Edges, and Polar Coordinates. Then try shaping and manipulating these patterns using various masks.

Monochromatic Noise

In Photoshop 3.0, the Noise dialog box includes the Monochromatic check box. This is an extremely useful option. If you randomly vary the brightness levels of pixels in color channels, the colors of the pixels will also change randomly. Often you only want to add noise to generate or modify tonal texture—not to generate or modify color. In Photoshop 2.5.1 you can accomplish this by adding noise to a floating selection, making a selection tool active, and choosing Luminosity in the Brushes palette, a roundabout but effective approach. In Photoshop 3.0 you can go to the Monochromatic check box and accomplish the same thing with the click of a button.

Banding

Banding is the breakup of smooth blends or gradients into visible bands of tone or color. This problem is the result of insufficient numbers of tones or colors in the image-reproduction system, a lack of natural noise in the image, or both. For years, digital images have been plagued by banding.

Regular photographs, which reproduce natural noise, seldom run into banding problems. Photographs that show clear blue sky and portraits with smooth wash lighting are notable and telling exceptions. Both these cases feature smooth images which, like synthetic computer blends, tend to show banding when printed on digital systems. To combat this problem, some Uniform noise was added to the sky in Figure 12.1.

Bands show up because our visual systems are very good at detecting minute shifts in tone or color. The eye can often find the bands even when the tone or color jumps are less than 0.5 percent. Bands in noise-free vertical and horizontal blends or gradients show up especially well (Figure 12.7). By adding some noise to the band regions, you can make the edges of the bands break up so that they become harder to detect (Figure 12.8).

Figure 12.7

The top window shows a 5 percent gradient from left to right, produced by the Gradient tool with no dithering. Depending on how much noise was added by the prepress and printing processes, you may or may not be able to detect the bands. In the bottom window, the same material has been expanded to full tonal range via Levels to show the bands clearly.

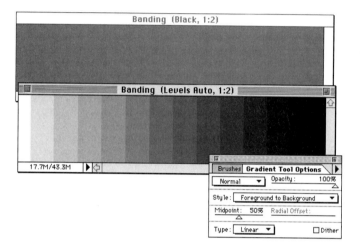

Figure 12.8

Adding noise to a gradient disrupts the clean band edges, making the tone or color transitions harder to detect. This illustration is the same as Figure 12.7, except that the Gradient Tool Options dither box was checked when the gradient was produced.

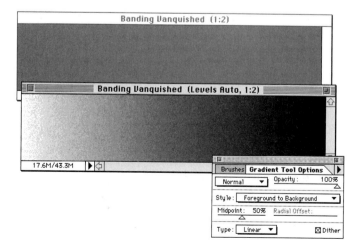

As Figures 12.7 and 12.8 illustrate, Photoshop 3.0's Gradient Tools Options palette offers a Dither checkbox for the automatic inclusion of noise in gradients as they are produced by the tool. If you need to add noise to an existing gradient or other very smooth area, try adding Uniform noise of Amount 5 for starters. Vary the amount of the noise until it is just slightly visible in a 1:1 view. Examine the appearance of the area in your final printed product to determine whether you need to use more or less noise the next time.

Get in the habit of including noise in the images you create entirely by computer. The images will print more reliably, and they'll probably have more vitality, too.

Noise and Apparent Sharpness

Noise has another talent: It can make certain types of images appear sharper to liven up their textures. This effect varies considerably from image to image, but a small amount of noise usually works best. Try adding uniform noise of 3 to 5 for starters, understanding that this is a quick-fix approach. For more elaborate sharpening Photoshop offers a range of tools including the Unsharp Mask filter, which is discussed next.

Blurring and Banding

Blurring spreads level variations among groups of pixels. Among its obvious uses in defocusing regions of images, it tends to make blends and gradients smoother. Ironically, this can also make banding worse. If you need to apply a blur for aesthetic reasons and the blurred region includes a blend or gradient, consider adding a little noise back into the region to minimize potential banding.

Sharpening

When you're trying to impress an audience, a nice sharp image helps. Unfortunately, many photographic images available in electronic form suffer from a slight softening of detail. To counteract this problem it's normal to sharpen virtually all photographic images somewhat, either as they are scanned or after the fact (Figure 12.9).

Figure 12.9
The 300-ppi image on the left was sharpened slightly during resampling. The image on the right was sharpened with Photoshop's Unsharp Mask filter, using an Amount of 100 percent, a Radius of 1.5 pixels, and a Threshold of 4 levels.

If you work with custom-scanned images from a high-end prepress shop, the sharpening should be done for you at scan time. If you work with other sources, such as CD-ROM images or scans from small desktop scanners, you'll often need to do some sharpening yourself.

Contrary to logic, the slight blurriness and lack of definition in scanned photographic images is not caused by a lack of sufficient image resolution, but by the processes of scanning, resizing, and halftoning. First of all, these processes average the image detail in various ways, which results in some loss. Second, even perfectly sharp images tend to look softer as their contrast is reduced due to the unavoidable tone compression that images suffer on the path from film to scanner to printing press. Third, conventional halftoning imposes a strict upper limit on reproducible detail.

Halftoning imposes a practical limit on resolution, because in a halftoned image you gain virtually no improvement in appearance from a resolution higher than two times the halftone screen lpi. For example, if you are printing with a 133 lpi halftone screen, you gain nothing once the resolution exceeds about 266 ppi. For many images, the improvements level off at a lower point, about 1.5 times the lpi.

Also, there's a difference between detail and sharpness. Detail is an intrinsic quality; an image either has detail or it doesn't. Sharpness, on the other hand, is a psychological quality relating to the perception of edges. With some special processing—sharpening—an image can often appear sharp even though it lacks detail.

If you'd like more information about sharpening after reading the rest of this chapter, refer to *Real World Halftoning and Scanning* (Peachpit Press, 1994). Authors Steve Roth and David Blatner explain the topic in detail from the viewpoint of the Photoshop user.

Sharpening Principles

Electronic scanners and computers aren't clairvoyant; they don't know about the detail that is missing from an image. All they can do is make the available detail stand out better by applying a standard edge-enhancement technique. This technique increases the tonal differences between adjacent pixels, which makes edges appear sharp (Figure 12.10).

Figure 12.10
Sharpening en-
hances available
image details by
increasing the
brightness differ-
ences between
pixels. This has
the effect of
making edges
look sharper
and textures
look grainier.

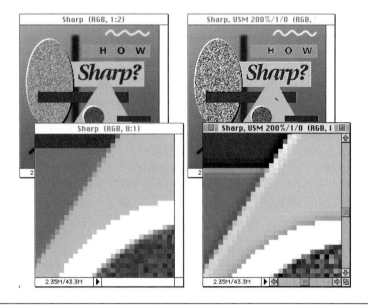

Sharpening relies on the subtle edge halos visible in the accompa-
nying figures. The key to successful sharpening is applying enough
of the effect to make the image look sharper, without applying
enough to make the halos evident to the viewer. Once the halos become visible, the image looks harsh.

Photoshop offers four sharpening filters, three of which—Sharpen,
Sharpen More, and Sharpen Edges—are one-shot effects that offer
no controls. In a surprising number of cases you might find that one
or more of these tools works well for you. The fourth filter, Unsharp
Mask, more than compensates for the lack of controls in the others
by providing very broad control of the three sharpening parameters:
radius, amount, and threshold. Each of these three parameters must
be set properly to achieve an acceptable result.

The sharpening Radius, set in pixels, adjusts the halo width (Figure
12.11). The Amount adjusts the depth of the added contrast within
the halos (Figure 12.12). The Threshold, expressed in brightness levels, allows you to exempt slight brightness changes—photographic

grain and other natural noise, for example—from sharpening. A Threshold setting of 4 to 6 levels often serves nicely to minimize the development of graininess during sharpening (Figure 12.13).

Figure 12.11
By adjusting the Unsharp Mask filter's Radius setting, you control the width of the halos that are necessary for the sharpening effect.

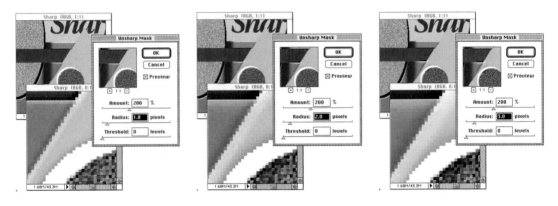

Figure 12.12
By adjusting the Unsharp Mask filter's Amount setting you vary the degree of contrast enhancement within the halo.

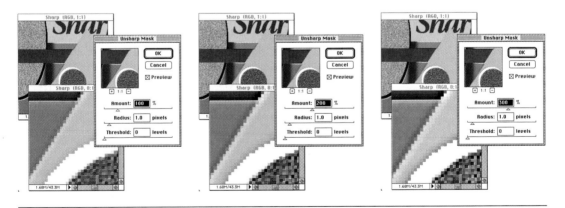

Figure 12.13
By adjusting the Unsharp Mask filter's Threshold setting, you can avoid sharpening subtle textures and photographic grain. (A small amount of Gaussian Noise was added to the image for this example.)

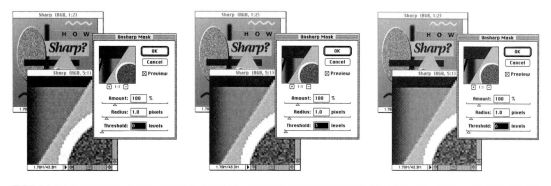

The best sharpening makes an image look right, neither frustratingly fuzzy or obviously processed. Your sharpening batting average will improve with practice, and there is no real substitute for seeing the image on a proof or in print.

Sharpening is tricky to gauge on your display screen. The halos should be just barely visible at the final reproduction size of the image. However, if you reduce the image to its approximate final size on your display you will usually end up viewing it in the 2:1, 3:1, or 4:1 view, which won't properly reproduce the halos. One possible approach is to display the image in a 1:1 view and stand back from the screen to judge the effect on at least a portion of the image. In any case, the image—assuming you can see it—should appear just slightly sharper than you would like, to compensate for the further softening that will occur during halftoning.

The new stochastic halftoning—which uses a dithering related to the bitmap dithers of Chapter 1—reproduces more image detail than does traditional halftoning. Thus, images reproduced with stochastic halftoning require less preparatory sharpening than the same images reproduced with conventional halftoning.

Applying the Sharpening Filters

Since the halo size is set in pixels (Radius), Photoshop's sharpening filters are resolution-dependent. As the pixel size decreases with increasing image resolution, so does the sharpening effect. You must adjust the Radius value to compensate. Since most Photoshop users work in circumstances where their images have a consistent range of resolutions, it's often possible to experiment and establish a few sharpening approaches that will produce reasonable results for the majority of images. For special cases you'll occasionally need to re-sharpen and process an image again, just like the prepress houses occasionally do.

Using the Unsharp Mask Filter

Author Steve Roth has come up with a handy formula for the Radius value: image resolution (in pixels per inch) divided by 200. This gives a halo width slightly narrower than a 1-point rule, which works well in most cases. According to the formula, an image with a resolution of 200 ppi should be sharpened with a Radius of 1 pixel, an image with a resolution of 300 ppi should be sharpened with a Radius of 1.5 pixel, and so on. The Unsharp Mask halos follow the same contour as the Gaussian Blur; in both cases the radius settings produce a wider effect than the numbers suggest.

To apply the filter, select a small but representative portion of the image as a test. (This filter takes a long time to run, so testing on a small area saves you time.) Determine the image's resolution, divide by 200, and set the Radius to this value. Applying the filter a few times with Amount settings of 75, 100, 150, and 200 percent will give you a good idea of the effect. Most images will require Radius and Amount settings in this range. Set the Threshold for a value of 3 to 6 for most images. All the numbers in this paragraph are starting suggestions only—every image is different. Still, in "normal" sharpening situations the majority of images require settings within these ranges (Figure 12.14).

Figure 12.14
Both of these 300-ppi images were sharpened with a Radius of 1.5 and a Threshold of 4. The Amount was 75 percent for the image on the left and 200 percent for the image on the right. Although neither of these Amount settings may be best for this particular image, a setting somewhere between these two extremes works well for most images. Compare these images with the right image of Figure 12.9, which uses the same Radius and Threshold settings with an amount of 100 percent.

Once you have established the Unsharp Mask setting using the small test area, apply the filter to the entire image (it may be prudent to sharpen a copy in case you decide to resharpen after seeing a proof).

Sharpening Tips and Notes

Sharpening is a topic that deserves a small book of its own, but here are a few additional tips and comments that may be helpful:

- Given the same image content, a slightly sharpened image of modest resolution looks sharper than an unsharpened image of high resolution (Figure 12.15).

Figure 12.15

A low-resolution image with a little sharpening looks sharper than a high-resolution image with none. The image on the left has a resolution of 600 ppi (far higher than needed for the 133 lpi screen used to print this book). The image on the right has a resolution of 200 ppi (1.5 times this book's 133 lpi), and it has also been sharpened using the Unsharp Mask filter with settings of Amount 75 percent, Radius 1, and Threshold 3.

- Make an image slightly sharper than you think it should be if you plan to use conventional halftoning, which softens images a bit.

- A little sharpening helps when images are reduced in size.

- Slightly increasing the contrast of the whole image, or even of just the area of primary visual interest, can give an impression of greater sharpness.

- Be wary of sharpening JPEG-compressed images. These images have compression-tile artifacts that excessive sharpening can bring out. The greater the compression, the more serious the tiling becomes.

- In a CMYK file, sharpening the Black channel alone is sometimes enough—assuming that there is material in the Black channel in the area that requires sharpening (check first).

- To counteract the softening that naturally results from image resampling, a slight sharpening is applied as part of Photoshop's Bicubic interpolation.

- One benefit of Photoshop's sharpening filters is that you can apply them to different portions of an image in different amounts as needed. When sharpening is done at scan time, the whole image receives the same sharpening.

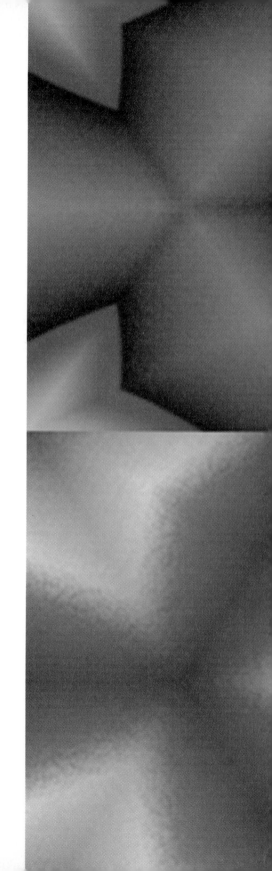

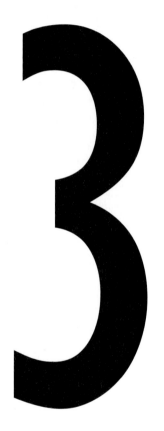

Using Textures
and Effects

CHAPTER

13

Textures

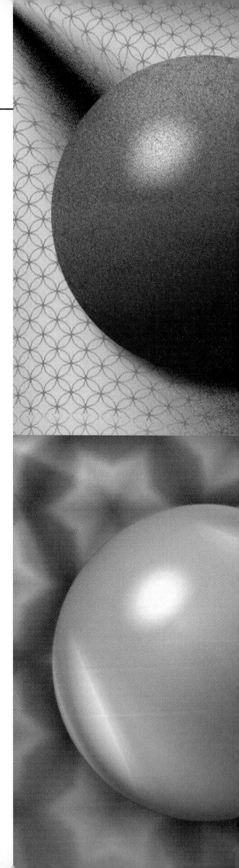

inally we touch on a very deep topic: textures. Textures give images a touch of realism, and mastery of texture techniques requires little more than practice, a willingness to experiment, and your own sense of what works. That said, the Photoshop texture terrain is vast and expanding so rapidly that you can't hope to master every tool and resource.

Given this, this chapter will help you think about textures and point you toward the minimum kit of texture tools you should have. As time goes on you will choose other tools as well, but you should regard the categories and filter sets mentioned here as the essentials.

This chapter progresses from the general to the specific. We begin with basic principles and categories, then discuss a few of the tools you should not be without.

Texture Basics

As noted in the previous chapter in Figure 12.2, if you use nothing more than Photoshop's painting tools it's easy to make electronic images that look flat, smooth, and lifeless. Texture puts interest and grit into an image. In the process, texture can also make an image behave better when you have to print it. The following section discusses some of the basic texture principles.

The Filter Marketplace

Texture tools consist largely of Photoshop's native filters, special third-party filters and programs, texture image sources, and the Photoshop commands used to modify images. Given the hundreds of filters and programs now available and the dozens of collections of CD-ROM textures, there's plenty to work with.

Third-party Photoshop filters fall into three general categories:

- Commercial packages from established firms
- Commercial packages from individuals
- Filters from amateurs

In general the packages from commercial firms are supported by teams of programmers, reasonably complete printed documentation, and technical support. Commercial programs from individuals tend to have less of these three advantages, and amateur filters are often uploaded to online services with only a cursory set of instructions, if anything. The quality and utility of filters tends to vary widely, but naturally the commercial packages from established firms have the edge.

With Photoshop 3.0, Adobe released a technical tool—Filter Factory—that will probably cause a sharp increase in the number of available filters. Filter Factory, a filter programming panel that appears in the filter menu, is intended more for the graphics programmer than the graphic artist. It makes the complex business of filter programming easier, and in the long run it should help make the filters better too.

Regardless of where you find filters or texture sources, some general principles apply when it comes to their use. These principles are discussed next.

Subtlety

Working with textures is as much an aesthetic activity as a technical one. As you experiment and practice, you'll come to appreciate subtlety. General tricks of the trade include using small amounts of effect, repeating and overlaying effects, and modifying effects with other effects.

Using Small Amounts of Effect

Among the major sins of electronic art is using too much effect, something commonly seen in galleries of Photoshop filter examples. Like a cook who uses too much spice, the artist with a heavy hand produces an obvious computer image. Try to see how little of an effect you can get by with. Apply the effect, then perform an immediate comparison with the Undo command, hitting Command+Z repeatedly to toggle the image before and after the effect to gauge the appearance. You'll often find that a small amount of an effect works just fine.

Repeating and Overlaying Effects

Just as a single stroke of a paintbrush seldom produces the effect an artist seeks, a single application of an electronic effect often fails to excite the heart. Repeated small applications, overlaid with a sense of exploration and taste, usually carry the day. You can sometimes dictate the amount of effect from within a filter. In other cases, you can make a selection, float it, and apply the effect. You can then turn the floating selection into a new layer—or simply vary the floating selection's opacity.

A useful trick with some textures is to apply a filter in a small amount, then hit Command+F to reapply the filter in small increments until you build up an effect to your taste. Keep in mind that your ability to undo an effect applied in this fashion will be limited, so save your file often.

Enhancement and Muting of Textures

Editing textures directly with texture-sensitive Photoshop commands and filters—especially blurring, sharpening, and edge effects—offers you a deeper range of textures. If a texture is almost smooth enough, almost gritty enough, or almost "textured" enough, you can usually use these tools to enhance it.

Serendipity

Rarely will you apply more than one or two textures in a row with a perfectly accurate idea of what the result will look like. With practice you'll learn what sorts of things to try, but you'll always be on firmer ground if you can try numerous effects and use the combination that best fits the needs of the image at hand. What shows up is often better than what you originally had in mind. As you become more familiar with the general appearance of various effects in combination, you'll learn how to encourage the right kinds of "accidents."

Used in concert, the above practices can help you build delightful, slightly unpredictable, and novel textures vital to interesting visuals.

Types of Textures

Textures come in many varieties. We'll group textures into four general categories—you might propose better ones, but these will serve for this discussion. My admittedly arbitrary texture categories are Grit, Patterns, Natural, and Abstract (Figure 13.1).

Grit

The random variation of life, the noise discussed in the previous chapter, takes forms that range from barely visible variations to obvious grime, sandpaper, stucco, mezzotints, and other grainy textures. Noise filters provide randomness, but you determine the degree to which this random noise is applied. Photoshop's Noise filter gives you the basic noise you need. Other filters are available and offer processed variations that can save you time and make exploration more productive.

Patterns

Many filters generate regular patterns. These patterns can often be stretched and otherwise distorted, tiled to fill an entire image, and

Figure 13.1
This chapter's arbitrary grouping places texture types into four broad categories: Grit (upper left), Patterns (upper right), Natural (lower left) and Abstract (lower right). Judicious combinations of these types often produce pleasing results.

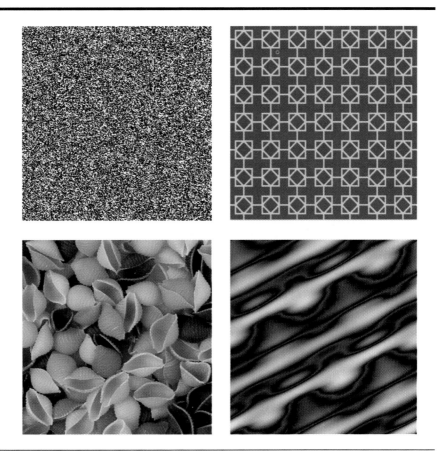

otherwise modified. There are also filters that help make patterns from segments of images.

Natural Textures

Everything from tree bark to granite, pond ripples, candy, and clouds in the sky—and anything else that can be photographed, for that matter—seems to be available on CD-ROM. The use of such material at first appears to be self-evident, but the possibilities are limited only by your imagination. There's no reason to stop with the "textures" material, of course. Nothing (except copyright limitations) should deter you from converting any appropriate portion of an image into a texture.

Abstract

Finally there are textures that grow from nothing other than mathematics. In the Photoshop environment all filters have a mathematical basis, grit and patterns included, but abstract filters add fractals and other artificial graphics to the list.

In practiced hands, abstract filters can generate apparently natural, near-natural, and supernatural textures. Surrealism comes naturally, but the filters offer many other possibilities.

Photoshop's Most Basic Texture Tools

Photoshop's Noise filter, in combination with the blur and sharpen filters, provides your most basic texture generator. In addition, almost all Photoshop filters can be used in one way or another to enhance these textures. Run various filters on noise, blurred noise, and sharpened blurred noise. Adjust the settings for these filters to get a good good "pure" look at what each filter can do, without having to contend with the effect the filter has on any specific image (Figure 13.2).

Third-Party Texture Tools

Of the many third-party texture products that work with Photoshop, four in particular have proven themselves in the areas of ongoing innovation, variety, and quality at the time this book is written. To be sure, other products perform certain specialized tasks better, and still others compete vigorously in various categories. Once you've become familiar with the terrain you might not agree with my choice of these four, but I believe at this time they constitute the basic third-party texture kit for the working Photoshop commercial artist.

Figure 13.2
Using just Photoshop's native filters you can create numerous textures. The key is to explore the capabilities before you need them, so you'll know what to do when you're on a deadline.

Andromeda Series Filters

Among the Andromeda Series 1 photographic special-effects filters is the Designs Filter (Figure 13.3), a pattern generator that provides useful starting points for complex textures. The rest of Series 1 features special-purpose filters that come in handy in specific circumstances.

The versatile Andromeda Series 2 filter deserves mention. While not a texture generator *per se*, this three-dimensional surface-mapping filter has become well regarded as a way to wrap textures around basic three-dimensional shapes. You can then apply various other filters to add to the textural richness or to distort the shapes.

Figure 13.3
The Andromeda
Series I filters,
in addition to
providing various
photographic
special effects, in-
clude the Designs
filter, a versatile
pattern generator.

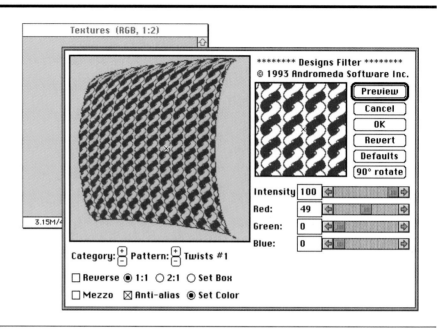

Xaos Tools

Xaos ("Chaos") Tools offers two useful filters, a texture generator and
a pattern generator that create patterns from part of an image. The
Paint Alchemy filter is discussed next, followed by a section on the
Terrazzo filter.

Xaos Tools Paint Alchemy

The Paint Alchemy filter (Figure 13.4) is a powerful texture generator. To make the filter operation easier to grasp, Xaos calls each of
the numerous filter settings a "brush," with the understanding that
when the filter is used the brush is applied dozens, hundreds or
thousands of times over the image, like some sort of magical paintbrush. The number of potential effects is essentially unlimited.

To make a powerful texture-generator filter commercially successful, it's a good idea to provide numerous presets for busy artists,
who work under deadlines that often don't allow the time to explore

Figure 13.4
The Xaos Tools Paint Alchemy filter provides dozens of easy-to-modify presets. The filter applies each "brush" numerous times over the image to build up a texture.

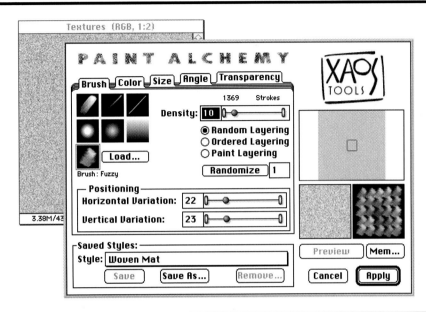

a filter's intricacies. Xaos, a company with a history in commercial computer graphics, has done an excellent job of preparing and distributing useful presets for the Paint Alchemy filter. In addition to the presets that come with the filter itself, Xaos also offers a "Floppy Full of Brushes," 50 additional presets. The filter also makes it easy to modify presets and preview the results.

Xaos Tools Terrazzo

The Terrazzo filter (Figure 13.5) brings the kaleidoscope concept to electronic production, building pattern tiles from material within a Photoshop selection. This allows you to quickly construct and preview complex patterns that use colors and shapes from the image on which you are currently working, or from other images as you wish.

The Terrazzo filter provides all the known tiling variations. As this is written the filter still has a few first-version quirks, but they are more than overcome by its usefulness.

Figure 13.5
The Xaos Tools Terrazzo filter makes it easy to create a practically infinite variety of tile patterns, using part of an image as source material.

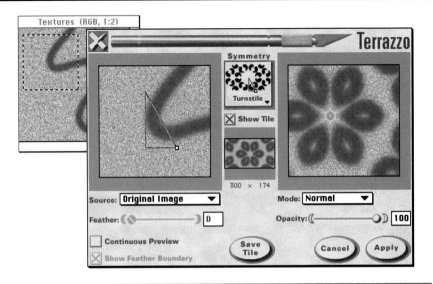

Kai's Power Tools (KPT)

If ever a set of filters was too versatile and powerful for its own good.... Well, let's just say that Kai's Power Tools from HSC Software—named for its principal creator, graphics visionary and time-traveler Kai Krause—is regarded by some people as reason enough to buy Adobe Photoshop. With both this set of filters and other advanced-but-affordable graphics products, the hypomanic gang from HSC Software has a habit of piling one tool on another, each tool cooler than the last.

Kai's Power Tools (often shortened to KPT) consists of more than three dozen filters that cover the ground from a simple selection-info filter to full-featured texture and fractal generator previewers. Just categorizing this assortment of filters is tough; I place them into the following three (admittedly arbitrary) major categories: handy one-shot effects, enhancements, and the four major modules.

Handy One-Shot Effects

These filters blur the line between abstract and artificial effects, offering one-click access to certain hard-to-generate effects. They include Glass Lens (Figure 13.6), Page Curl, Vortex Tiling, and Stereo Noise.

Figure 13.6
Variations on a basic theme, using the KPT Glass Lens filter to make the sphere. The Andromeda Series 1 Designs filter created the pattern for the background at upper right, and the Xaos Tools Terrazzo filter created the tiling patterns at the lower right, one of which is used in the image background at lower left.

Enhancements

Another category of KPT filters offers tasteful enhancements of basic Photoshop filter effects, mostly of the grit variety. This category includes numerous special noise filters, tone-enhancement filters, and special-purpose smudge filters.

The Major Modules

The four major modules—two gradient modules, a texture explorer, and a fractal explorer—stand as separate mini-applications of their own. All modules offer numerous presets and a way to save and recall your own settings.

The Gradient Designer and Gradients on Paths   The Gradient Designer (Figure 13.7) offers a way to build, store, and modify complex abstract gradients, saving a great deal of time when you need a special metallic look, for example, or a rainbow of colors with a couple of folds in the middle. The companion Gradients on Paths (Figure 13.8) lets you apply gradients within the feathered region of a selection, a handy way to wrap a gradient in a loop.

Figure 13.7
Like the other four major KPT modules, the Gradient Designer lets you build complex gradients. You can also rely on the numerous presets. Many functions and choices are located in hidden pop-up menus.

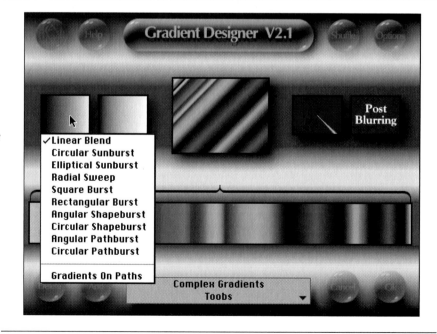

Figure 13.8
The KPT Gradients on Paths filter lets you wrap the Gradient Designer's gradients around shapes. This filter is applied to the feathered region of selections.

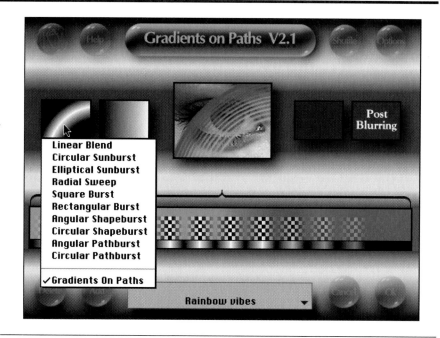

The Texture Explorer

The Texture Explorer (Figure 13.9) generates abstract patterns of great variety, and offers an elegant system for working your way toward a texture you like. Some textures are realistic enough to use in standard commercial work without raising a client's suspicions, and they are royalty-free, of course.

The Fractal Explorer

For serious fractal hounds and graphics wanderers, the Fractal Explorer offers the ultimate in mathematical abstract graphics. Used tastefully in small amounts, fractals can be very powerful in conventional images. On the other hand, when you need something truly surreal, fractals are a great place to begin. Again there is an elegant exploration interface and a convenient way to save your settings.

Figure 13.9
Once you spend about a half hour learning the KPT Texture Explorer interface, you can quickly examine hundreds of abstract textures, temporarily protecting those you like (in the small red frames). A similar half-hour learning period is needed to gain basic competence in all four major modules.

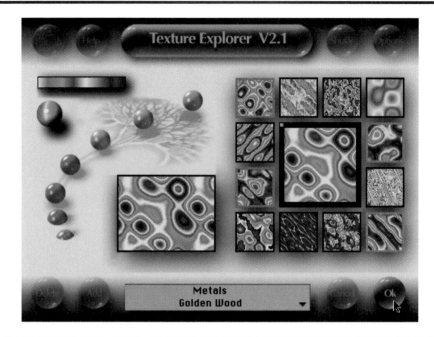

KPT Challenges

Now to recognize a few challenges that accompany this astonishingly powerful set of tools, followed by some simple remedies.

First, Kai's Power Tools was not initially designed with high production volume in mind. You won't be alone if you feel overwhelmed by this powerful set of filters. Designed by extremely intelligent people who live to explore and who thrive on the creative possibilities of serendipity, the major modules' interfaces encourage exploration. This philosophy has generated a package in which labels for some of the controls are consciously omitted, and some critical functions for some of the filters are hidden, leaving you to "discover" them. Unfortunately, being forced to explore can prove quite frustrating for the commercial artist on a deadline—you might love to browse, but in reality you can afford only minutes to find an effect you can use.

Second, since many people who make commercial art need to work fast, and because many haven't taken time to understand the filters, they tend to use certain commercial-looking presets without much adjustment. As a result, a "KPT look" has emerged from the application of a dozen or so overused effects, gradients, and textures. There's no need for this, because the filters can generate far more effects than are represented by presets.

Finally, there's the mining factor—the presets you need for any given project can be nuggets among a mass of ore. The presets offer such a wide range of gradients and textures that only a few are appropriate for any given need, but still you must hunt through hundreds of their whimsically named relatives.

Navigating in KPT

All of the above concerns boil down to two issues: navigation and organization. If you're willing to invest four or five hours in these areas you'll use KPT filters with assurance. I'll cover navigation first.

You can get a huge amount of work done with KPT even if you don't know how to use it well, but you do have to know how to find your way around. Invest a couple of hours learning how to get around the gradient, texture, and fractal modules and another hour or two reviewing the one-shot filters. You'll learn enough during this time to accommodate many commercial needs well. Concentrate your early efforts on learning how to review a lot of material—you can create new presets later on. For the one-shot filters, set aside ten minutes to read the KPT manual and experiment with each filter.

Here are some key tips for the four major modules, some of them drawn right from the KPT manual:

- Set aside a half-hour to read the manual and study each module's operation. Since the buttons are unlabeled, get a feel for what they do. Also read where to click; certain critical functions are available by clicking on preview windows, for example.

- The up-arrow and down-arrow keys step through the presets. You can hold your finger down on either of them and quickly see dozens of presets. The Page Up and Page Down keys move you between whole preset categories.

- The left-arrow and right-arrow keys step through color variations in the Texture Explorer and Fractal Explorer. In combination with the up-arrow and down-arrow keys, this puts hundreds of variations at your fingertips in these modules.

- Click on the Shuffle button to see many more variations.

- Always click and hold the Option button to check the apply modes, which work like Photoshop's. If you have a great texture you want to apply to a white background, you won't get very far by applying it in Lighten mode, for example. The apply mode is determined separately in every preset, and often is set to something you don't want. Check it before you click on OK.

- Get in the habit of applying the filters to floating selections. You can then turn the floating selection into a layer, where you can keep working with it.

- If you see a texture or gradient you like but the color is wrong, use it anyway—then adjust the color with the Hue/Saturation command or other Photoshop editing functions.

Organize the Presets

Once you find that preset you like, save it where you can find it fast! The Add button lets you establish new categories and presets (Figures 13.10 and 13.11). Name the presets you like in a way that makes sense to you. You can also clean up the other presets by deleting ones you've saved under other names—although this can be risky. Be careful not to delete the gradient presets that feed other presets in the Texture Explorer and Fractal Explorer.

Figure 13.10
The organization and naming of the default KPT gradient, texture, and fractal presets can seem whimsical to a commercial artist, and can make it harder to find what you want. This illustration shows some of the most conservative preset names.

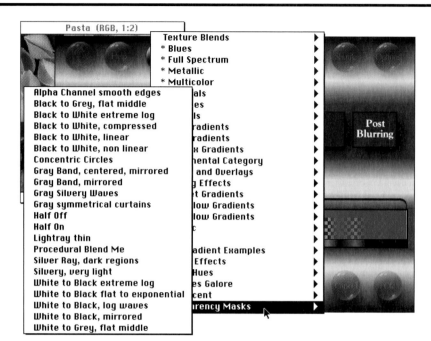

Figure 13.11
Here's an easy solution to the problem shown in Figure 13.10—give your favorite presets names meaningful to you, and place them in your own new categories. In this illustration, my new categories begin with asterisks, and the preset names follow my own system.

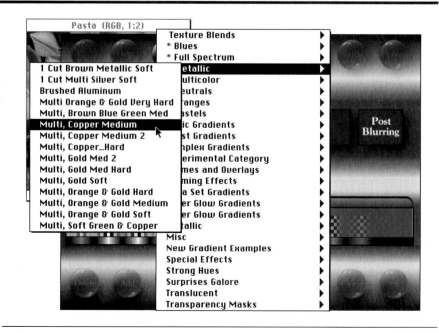

Your presets are saved in the KPT User Presets file in the KPT Support Files folder, which is located in your Photoshop Plug-ins folder.

PhotoDisc and Other CD-ROMs

If you prefer to obtain your textures ready-made on CD-ROM, there are numerous collections you can use. Don't miss the opportunity to adjust their colors, tone, and texture with Photoshop's editing functions.

As the CD-ROM universe keeps expanding, the lines between literal and artificial textures are blurring. Fresco (Figure 13.12), an interesting CD-ROM from Xaos Tools, offers expertly created Paint Alchemy textures, ready to open as images. Among the many CD-ROM image collections, the PhotoDisc line offers a good basic library of images you can use royalty-free once you've purchased the discs (Figure 13.13).

Figure 13.12
In addition to the Paint Alchemy filters, Xaos Tools offers the Fresco CD-ROM, which contains ready-to-use images created by the firm's own Paint Alchemy experts.

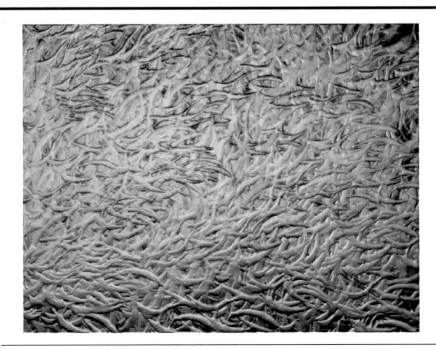

Figure 13.13
An endless supply of textures is available on CD-ROM. One of the best collections of royalty-free images is the PhotoDisc series, which offers everything from candy to clouds.

Third-Party Vendor Contact Information

The third-party vendors in this chapter contributed samples for use in this book, but that isn't why they're covered here—we approached them first because of their excellent reputations. Think of these products as just the beginning; other top-rate suppliers of related graphics products will emerge. As the explosive growth of this industry proves time and again, you should always keep your eyes open for the newcomers.

For additional information on filters and textures, Bill Niffenegger's book *Photoshop Filter Finesse* (Random House) offers a solid overview of what's available in late 1994.

Here is where you can obtain the products mentioned in this chapter:

Andromeda Series Filters
Andromeda Software Inc.
699 Hampshire Rd., Suite 109
Westlake Village, CA 91361
805-379-4109

Kai's Power Tools
HSC Software
6303 Carpinteria Avenue
Carpinteria, CA 93013
805-566-6200

PhotoDisc
2013 Fourth Avenue, Suite 402
Seattle, WA 98121
206-441-9355

Paint Alchemy and Terrazzo
Xaos Tools
600 Townsend, Suite 270 East
San Francisco, CA 94103
415-487-7000

INDEX

Index **217**

U

V

X

sources of, 191–192, 196–210
types of, 194–196
third-party filters, 192, 196–210
This Layer sliders, 52–53
tones and masks containing, 22–24
Transparency mask, 56, 57–59
for drop shadows, 117
saving to alpha channel, 59
transparency versus opacity, 56
trapping, 134–136
Type tool, 31

U

Underlying sliders, 53
Undo command, 193
Uniform noise, 172–175, 178
Unsharp Mask filter, 178, 182–183, 184–185

V

vector graphics, 135–136
versus pixel graphics, 4–5
Vortex Tiling (KPT) filter, 201

X

x and y coordinates (addresses of pixels), 7, 14
Xaos Tools filters, 210
Paint Alchemy, 198–199
Terrazzo, 199–200

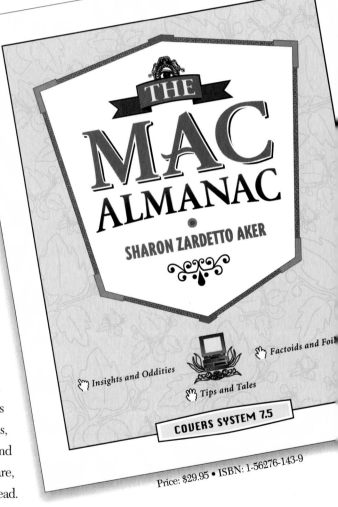

Ride the Fast Lane on the Information Highway

with Ziff-Davis Press.

Driving lessons for online newcomers.
The latest waves for expert net surfers.

In these just-released books from Ziff-Davis Press, noted authors share their passion for the online world. Join them on a thrilling ride down the information highway from the comfort of your home or office.

THE INTERNET VIA MOSAIC AND WORLD-WIDE WEB

$24.95 ISBN: 1-56276-259-1

PC Magazine UK Labs Manager Steve Browne focuses on Mosaic, the most popular Web browser. Browne concisely explains how to gain access to the Web and how to take advantage of the Web's hyper-linked environment through Mosaic. Included are valuable discussions on the ways business can take advantage of the Web.

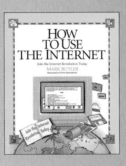

HOW TO USE THE INTERNET

$17.95 ISBN: 1-56276-222-2

Colorfully illustrated how-to guide; the easiest way for beginning Internet users to have fun and get productive fast.

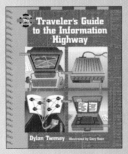

THE TRAVELER'S GUIDE TO THE INFORMATION HIGHWAY

$24.95 ISBN: 1-56276-206-0

The ultimate atlas to online resources including CompuServe, America Online, the Internet, and more.

THE INTERNET BY E-MAIL

$19.95 ISBN: 1-56276-240-0

Fun and informative Internet services available at no extra charge from the e-mail system you already know.

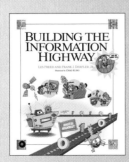

BUILDING THE INFORMATION HIGHWAY

$24.95 ISBN: 1-56276-126-9

Our present and future information structure, delightfully illustrated and clearly explained for anyone who's curious.

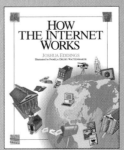

HOW THE INTERNET WORKS

$24.95 ISBN: 1-56276-192-7

Best-selling, full-color presentation of the technological marvel that links people and communities throughout the world.

Click, Click,

PC/Computing
How Computers Work
CD-ROM/Book
extravaganza
from
Ziff-Davis Press.

W H I Z

Click your way through an electrifying multimedia voyage to the heart of the computer with *How Multimedia Computers Work*—a unique CD-ROM packaged with the classic best-selling book *PC/Computing How Computers Work*.

In *How Multimedia Computers Work*, fun, fast-paced,

fascinating tours of your computer's incredible innards combine state-of-the-art 3D animation with lively dialog and music for a richly interactive sensory feast. Also included are provocative video interviews

with well-known computer industry figures—plus tons of computing tips from the top authors at Ziff-Davis Press. Teamed up with a book that has already shown legions

of computer users what makes their machine tick, *How Multimedia Computers Work* is a real whiz-bang experience that's sure to make you see your computer in a whole new light.

HOW COMPUTERS WORK

INCLUDES INTERACTIVE CD-ROM

NEW YORK FESTIVALS
GOLD MEDAL WINNER
1994
FOR PC/COMPUTING HOW MULTIMEDIA COMPUTERS WORK CD-ROM

BESTSELLER

RON WHITE
Illustrated by TIMOTHY EDWARD DOWNS

ISBN: 1-56276-250-8   Price: $39.95

BANG

Ziff-Davis Press Survey of Readers

Please help us in our effort to produce the best books on personal computing.
For your assistance, we would be pleased to send you a FREE catalog
featuring the complete line of Ziff-Davis Press books.

1. How did you first learn about this book?

Recommended by a friend . . . . ☐ -1 (5)
Recommended by store personnel . . . . ☐ -2
Saw in Ziff-Davis Press catalog . . . . ☐ -3
Received advertisement in the mail . . . . ☐ -4
Saw the book on bookshelf at store . . . . ☐ -5
Read book review in: _____ ☐ -6
Saw an advertisement in: _____ ☐ -7
Other (Please specify): _____ ☐ -8

2. Which THREE of the following factors most influenced your decision to purchase this book? (Please check up to THREE.)

Front or back cover information on book . . . ☐ -1 (6)
Logo of magazine affiliated with book . . . . . . ☐ -2
Special approach to the content . . . . ☐ -3
Completeness of content . . . . ☐ -4
Author's reputation. ☐ -5
Publisher's reputation . . . . ☐ -6
Book cover design or layout . . . . ☐ -7
Index or table of contents of book . . . . ☐ -8
Price of book . . . . ☐ -9
Special effects, graphics, illustrations . . . . . . ☐ -0
Other (Please specify): _____ ☐ -x

3. How many computer books have you purchased in the last six months? _____ (7-10)

4. On a scale of 1 to 5, where 5 is excellent, 4 is above average, 3 is average, 2 is below average, and 1 is poor, please rate each of the following aspects of this book below. (Please circle your answer.)

Depth/completeness of coverage	5	4	3	2	1	(11)
Organization of material	5	4	3	2	1	(12)
Ease of finding topic	5	4	3	2	1	(13)
Special features/time saving tips	5	4	3	2	1	(14)
Appropriate level of writing	5	4	3	2	1	(15)
Usefulness of table of contents	5	4	3	2	1	(16)
Usefulness of index	5	4	3	2	1	(17)
Usefulness of accompanying disk	5	4	3	2	1	(18)
Usefulness of illustrations/graphics	5	4	3	2	1	(19)
Cover design and attractiveness	5	4	3	2	1	(20)
Overall design and layout of book	5	4	3	2	1	(21)
Overall satisfaction with book	5	4	3	2	1	(22)

5. Which of the following computer publications do you read regularly; that is, 3 out of 4 issues?

Byte . . . . ☐ -1 (23)
Computer Shopper . . . . ☐ -2
Home Office Computing . . . . ☐ -3
Dr. Dobb's Journal . . . . ☐ -4
LAN Magazine . . . . ☐ -5
MacWEEK . . . . ☐ -6
MacUser . . . . ☐ -7
PC Computing . . . . ☐ -8
PC Magazine . . . . ☐ -9
PC WEEK . . . . ☐ -0
Windows Sources . . . . ☐ -x
Other (Please specify): _____ ☐ -y

Please turn page.

6. What is your level of experience with personal computers? With the subject of this book?

	With PCs	With subject of book
Beginner.	☐ -1 (24)	☐ -1 (25)
Intermediate.	☐ -2	☐ -2
Advanced.	☐ -3	☐ -3

7. Which of the following best describes your job title?

Officer (CEO/President/VP/owner). . . . . ☐ -1 (26)
Director/head. . . . . ☐ -2
Manager/supervisor. . . . . ☐ -3
Administration/staff. ☐ -4
Teacher/educator/trainer. . . . . ☐ -5
Lawyer/doctor/medical professional. . . . . . . ☐ -6
Engineer/technician. . . . . ☐ -7
Consultant. . . . . ☐ -8
Not employed/student/retired. . . . . ☐ -9
Other (Please specify): _____ ☐ -0

8. What is your age?

Under 20. . . . . ☐ -1 (27)
21-29. . . . . ☐ -2
30-39. . . . . ☐ -3
40-49. . . . . ☐ -4
50-59. . . . . ☐ -5
60 or over. . . . . ☐ -6

9. Are you:

Male. . . . . ☐ -1 (28)
Female. . . . . ☐ -2

Thank you for your assistance with this important information! Please write your address below to receive our free catalog.

Name: _____

Address: _____

City/State/Zip: _____

Fold here to mail.   2737-11-17

_____

_____

_____

BUSINESS REPLY MAIL
FIRST CLASS MAIL   PERMIT NO. 1612   OAKLAND, CA

POSTAGE WILL BE PAID BY ADDRESSEE

Ziff-Davis Press
5903 Christie Avenue
Emeryville, CA 94608-1925
Attn: Marketing

NO POSTAGE
NECESSARY
IF MAILED IN
THE UNITED
STATES

Peter's Image Recipes™

See this book's techniques applied in step-by-step fashion, on your screen and in a handy booklet!

Peter's Image Recipes are available for **Photoshop 2.5 and Photoshop 3.0.** A sample recipe is shown at right. Call the toll-free number below for complete recipe information, and see the other side of this page for more.

Peter Fink and Fresh Paint offer seminars, videotapes, and Peter's Image Recipes™ to help professionals learn to use Adobe Photoshop efficiently. Give us a call and we'll send you complete information on these products.

Fresh Paint
Incorporated
Arlington, Virginia

800-551-5921

Round Stone 1   Volume One for 2.5.1

Variations: Different backgrounds, vary amounts of Noise and Blur, vary depth of roundness and drop shadow tones with Levels, airbrush highlights to taste.

1 Create an image with a color blend. Add a new channel; name it Master. Select a dingbat character you like, adjust its point size and place it in Master, fine-tuning its position to taste. Return to Cmd-0 view, Load Master, and fill the selection with a light gray. Don't deselect yet…

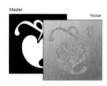

2 Float the selection, add Noise to taste (try Gaussian noise of about 75), and use Luminosity in the Composite Controls dialog to make the noise gray-only. (You can also use Luminosity in the Brushes palette if you have a selection tool active).Now drop the selection.

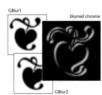

3 Duplicate the Master channel. Invert and apply a Gaussian Blur to the new channel, offset it to the upper left, and name it GBlur1. Duplicate channel GBlur1, offset the duplicate to the lower right, and name it GBlur2. Do a Difference calculation on GBlur 1 and GBlur2, to create a blurred chrome mask.

4 Trim the edge of the blurred chrome mask by performing a Multiply calculation with the Master channel. (First make sure the Master channel is light on dark.) Name the result Chrome.

5 Load the Chrome Mask and darken the selected areas to produce a roundness effect. You can do this by filling with black, but for more control you can use Levels. Experiment with Input and Output sliders in the Levels dialog box until you get an effect you like.

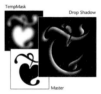

6 To create a drop shadow, first make a TempMask by duplicating Master, applying a Gaussian Blur, offsetting, then inverting as necessary to make TempMask light on dark as shown at left. Make sure Master is dark on light, then Multiply Master by TempMask. Name the result Drop Shadow.

Round Stone 1 (Continued)   Volume One for 2.5.1

7 Load the Drop Shadow mask and, as in Step 5, darken the selected areas with a fill of black, or use Levels for better control. Now your image seems to float, and has more cues about the light. You can vary the blur and offset amounts for different amounts of "float" and apparent light diffusion.

8 (Optional exploration) By varying the blurring and offset as you make a drop shadow mask, you can completely control the shadow. Make a few different drop shadow masks and try them out as in Step 9. (With similar adjustments to GBlur1 and GBlur2, you can vary the roundness in the chrome mask.)

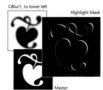

9 Now make a mask to use for airbrushing highlight accents. First, consider the direction of the light (your drop shadow gives the cues). Then offset GBlur 1 accordingly and Multiply by Master. The light in this image is to the upper right, so offset GBlur 1 to the lower left before multiplying.

10 Load the new highlight mask and airbrush the accents. You will have more control if you use a low airbrush opacity and build up the accents gradually. Try painting with white at about 5% opacity.

11 For an optional final touch, load the Master mask one last time and airbrush a wide highlight swath at a low opacity, moving the airbrush in the direction of the arrow. This technique often requires a few tries (followed by Undo's) until the effect finally looks right.

Voilá!
Try this recipe with various textures in the background and foreground, various amounts of blurring and offsets in the intermediate masks for the Chrome, Drop Shadow, and Highlight masks, and various airbrush accents. It's a tasty delight you can use in many settings!

See more info on the other side of this page!

See this book in action!

Watch Peter Fink create the images on this page using the techniques described in this unique book.

Peter Fink and Fresh Paint offer seminars, videotapes, and Peter's Image Recipes™ to help professionals learn to use Adobe Photoshop efficiently. Give us a call and we'll send you complete information on these products.

Fresh Paint Incorporated
Arlington, Virginia

800-551-5921

See more info on the other side of this page!